MW00718390

Developed to track individual diet and exercise plans for eight weeks

The Workout Notebook

Plus diet, attitude, & exercise tips

By

Karen Madrid

Published by

BARCLAY BOOKS, LLC

Barclay Books, LLC
St. Petersburg, FL

I dedicate this book to everyone who tries!

I'd like to thank my family for their patience and "diet" support over the last 17 years.

ISBN: 1-931402-06-X

Published by Barclay Books
Cover by Karen Madrid

Contents

Introduction

I developed *The Workout Notebook* when I got serious about my exercise and diet program, and I was without an organized way of tracking my progress. Until then, I had relied upon the latest fad diets and exercise programs as guides and, frankly, the results had always been a lack of energy and an unhealthy condition. So, after the latest fad diet failure, I decided to do my own research, and this notebook is a result of that effort. By actually using my process for more than a year now, the notebook is well tested and simplified!

The concept I used when developing *The Workout Notebook* is based upon the USDA's food pyramid and the Surgeon General's advice that daily exercise is crucial for optimum health. In addition, the notebook contains the good advice of trainers and diet experts, as well as my own personal experience.

Below is the information I used to develop *The Workout Notebook.*

USDA recommends a balanced daily diet. Their site has extensive, easy to read information. All brought to you buy your tax dollar!
Web page: http://www.usda.gov

Food Group	Daily Serving Amount
Fats/Oils/Sweets – Butter, chocolate, jellies	Sparingly
Dairy – Milk, cheese, yogurt	2 to 3 servings
Fruits – bananas, oranges, tomatoes	2 to 4 servings
Protein – Beans, eggs, chicken, beef	2 to 3 servings
Vegetables – carrots, corn, squash	3 to 5 servings
Whole Grains – rice, oatmeal, wheat	6 to 11 servings
Water	8 to 10 cups per day

The Surgeon General Physical Activity Report, 1996, recommends daily activity.

Web page: http://www.osophs.dhhs.gov/sgoffice.htm

- Physical activity need not be strenuous to achieve health benefits.
- Men and women of all ages benefit from a moderate amount of daily physical activity. The same moderate amount of activity can be obtained in longer sessions of moderately intense activities (such as 30 minutes of brisk walking) or in shorter sessions of more strenuous activities (such as 15-20 minutes of jogging).
- Additional health benefits can be gained through greater amounts of physical activity. Adults who maintain a regular routine of physical activity that is of longer duration or of greater intensity are likely to derive greater benefit. However, because risk of injury also increases with greater amounts of activity, care should be taken to avoid excessive amounts.
- Previously sedentary people who begin physical activity programs should start with short sessions (5-10 minutes) of physical activity and gradually build up to the desired level of activity.
- Adults with chronic health problems, such as heart disease, diabetes, or obesity, or who are at high risk for these conditions should first consult a physician before beginning a new program of physical activity. Men over age 40 and women over age 50 who plan to begin a new program of **vigorous** activity should consult a physician to be sure they do not have heart disease or other health problems.

Pretty simple, huh? The process I designed is based solely upon this information.

Okay. Now for an explanation of the "guts" in this book. Inside are eight weeks of two tables that have developed a healthy life style for a full-time working wife and mother. I got tired of diet and exercise plans that took up too much time with thinking and the end result was always "my butt is still big."

The Diet table provides serving sizes, examples of foods for that particular food group, and blocks to track your consumption. You can track either by a checkmark per serving or write down the calories and add them up. If you've never dieted before, just follow the USDA's recommended servings per day of each food group and you will be eating a healthy balanced diet.

The Exercise table provides tracking blocks for cardio, weight lifting, and do-at-home exercises. There are even some blank blocks so you can track an exercise I've missed!

The book also provides a Progress Chart so you'll never lose those measurements again. The Diet, Attitude, and Exercise Tips give you the suggestions I find to be the most important when beginning a new program. The Calorie Table lists food calories, and there is space for you to add more. I put in a table of exercises and the calories burned when doing them for an hour. All this info can be found while surfing the Internet. The Power Food Table, taken from the *Muscle & Fitness Magazine*, is to give you ideas for choosing foods that provide good nutrition.

Persons training for an athletic event can also use ***The Workout Notebook***. It has the ability to be used in planning your diet strategy and scheduling your workout routine for optimum performance.

I know this notebook works because, for the first time in 17 years, my diet isn't starving me, my workout isn't killing me, and I am successfully persuading my butt to come back from visiting my thighs!

So, let's get started! ***The Workout Notebook*** will work for you, because how can you fail when you begin?

Progress Chart

The Progress Chart tracks your weight and major body measurements. During the course of every diet and exercise program, you will not only lose weight, but you will lose inches. This chart will keep track of both. So, break out the scale and tape measure, turn the page, and start taking those measurements. Make sure to write down the day of the week that you measure.

Progress Chart

Day of the Week for Weigh In: _____

	Week 1	Week 2	Week 3	Week 4
Date				
Weight				
Neck				
Chest				
Waist				
Hips				
Arm				
Thigh				
Calf				
	Week 5	Week 6	Week 7	Week 8
Date				
Weight				
Neck				
Chest				
Waist				
Hips				
Arm				
Thigh				
Calf				

Instructions

Open the book in the middle and you will find eight weeks worth of diet and exercise tracking pages. Why eight weeks? Because theory has it that, if a person performs a task for approximately 20 days, a habit can be formed. So why not eight weeks worth? And eight weeks is when I begin to notice changes! Below, are the instructions on filling them out. If you are still confused, contact me at **madridka@aol.com** and I'll help you!

The book is also supported with a website at: http://**communities.msn.com/workoutnotebook**.

Daily Diet Page

The diet page table contains blocks for each food group and "servings per day" recommendations as set up by the USDA. The line underneath contains a quantity of that food group which equals one serving.

Easy Method

I suggest that beginners use this method. Begin with tracking your current routine for a week. This is an easy way to develop the habit of tracking what you are eating each day. You will naturally start making changes because you will notice what food groups you are not eating and whoa…. How many snacks did I eat today? Writing down the calories will take more time, as will adding them up. I don't want you to become discouraged because you think it's too complicated. Once you establish the habit, you will naturally ask, "How many calories am I eating?" And so will begin the habit of writing them down and adding them up. I will use several different methods during the week, based upon my time. Sometimes I just don't care about counting calories! The point of tracking is to develop the habit of selecting food from a variety of sources.

Instructions for the Easy Method

- Write in the date in the date block.

- When you eat a food group, put a checkmark in the block under the appropriate food group. Example: If you eat an egg and cheese sandwich, you would put one check mark for each egg under the Meat Group, one checkmark for each slice of bread under the Whole Grains, and one checkmark for each slice of cheese under Dairy Products. At the end of the day, you will tally up your checkmarks for that food group and write it in the "Total" block. By knowing what the USDA recommends, you are able to adjust your diet accordingly. Ensuring you are eating something from each food group in the correct proportion, assures a healthy balanced diet. Too easy?

Here's an example of the checkmark method:

Vegetables (3-5 Servings)								Servings Per Week/Day:	
1 piece, 1 cup raw, 1/2 cup canned, 1 oz dried, 6 oz juice								Fat	
✓	✓	✓	✓					Total	4

Remember to keep track of all those trips to the vending machine and the handfuls of chips you eat while passing by the kitchen! I use a checkmark for each handful. You'll be amazed at how many "little" snacks you eat. Just cutting those out will decrease your calorie intake!

Simple Method

When you get good at check-marking your diet, you can start keeping track of calories. Each food has a certain amount of calories. A calorie is the amount of heat required to raise the temperature of 1 kilogram of water 1 degree Celsius. What?? If you eat "x" number of calories, then your body requires "y" amount of energy to burn them. If you eat more calories than you burn, the body converts the extra calories into fat and stores it ~ usually in a place we don't even want to talk about!

To keep track of your calories, instead of putting a checkmark in the block, write in the calories. You can find the calories per serving on food labels. Here is an example of a food label. You can also find some basic food calories on the "Table of Calories" in the back of this book.

At the end of the day, instead of adding up checkmarks, add up the calories for each food group, and then add all the food groups together. Now you will be able to track how many calories a day you are eating. Here's an example:

Grain Group – 6 servings per day
Bread, Pasta, Oatmeal, Cereal, Muffin, Bagel, Rice, Tortilla

1 slice bread, 1/2 muffin/bun/bagel/tortilla, 1/2 c. pasta/rice, 1oz b/fast cereal								Total	
100	70	70	120	70	70				500

Did you notice next to the calories, it said "calories from fat?" On this example, 15 of the 60 calories come from the fat group. You can keep track of your fat calories on your chart, too. Look at the example below.

Grain Group – 6 servings per day
Bread, Pasta, Oatmeal, Cereal, Muffin, Bagel, Rice, Tortilla

1 slice bread, 1/2 muffin/bun/bagel/tortilla, 1/2 c. pasta/rice, 1oz b/fast cereal								Total	
70/15	70/10	70/10	80/20	70/10	70/10				430/75

Why is this important? Look at the chart below.

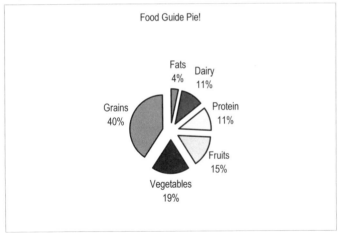

Food Guide Pie!

This chart breaks down the food pyramid into percentages. If a person is on a 1300 calorie a day diet, you can use this chart to figure out how many calories should come from each food group.

Food Group	Percent	Calories per Group
Fats	4	52
Dairy	11	143
Meat	11	143
Fruits	15	195
Vegetables	19	247
Grains	40	520
Totals	100	1300

If you didn't write down any calories in the fats & sweets group, and think you did great on that block, keeping track of your fat calories will make you take notice that you are getting your fat from other food groups. A cup of rice has 0 fat calories, while a slice of bread can have up to 20 calories from fat. That is why it is better to eat rice for your grains group than 6 slices of bread! Make sure to choose good food for your different groups.

Advanced Method

Are you ready to play the game for real? This method will require **pre-planning time** and some basic math skills, so break out the calculator and let's get started. _If you don't have time, please do the formulas just so you'll understand how calorie intake, calorie burning, and fat storage affect your weight loss goals._ You won't be so discouraged if your weight isn't coming off as fast as you planned! It may just be a matter of math.

If you do have time for this method, I suggest you start your diet plan with the easy method first, then the simple method, and hit this method last. Two reasons ~ you don't want to become discouraged as you start a new diet plan, and this section requires information from the simple method. Track the simple method for two weeks, and then try this method.

Okay ~ let's do some math and figure out how your body works with the intake of food and the burning of calories. Using this process, you can estimate your weight gain and loss, and find an understanding as to why those last 10 pounds to lose are the WORST!

First, let's figure out how many calories (or food intake) a day a person needs to maintain their current body weight with the amount of activity they do.

Take your current weight and multiply it by an activity multiplier. Here's an explanation of each activity multiplier. Which one do you fall under?

Multiplier	Activity Level
10	None – sit and watch TV
13.6	Exercise at least twice a week for an hour
16-18	Exercise 3 to 4 times a week – sports or gym activity
20	Exercises enough to sweat for an hour every day

Do all the formulas below, using your weight, so you can see the differences in the activity levels.

_____ ×   10   = _____
Weight   Activity Multiplier   Calories Required

_____ ×   13.6   = _____
Weight   Activity Multiplier   Calories Required

_____ ×   16   = _____
Weight   Activity Multiplier   Calories Required

_____ ×   20   = _____
Weight   Activity Multiplier   Calories Required

Circle the calories that you require to maintain your current body weight.

Use the following to figure out how many calories will be needed as you lose weight. Use a constant activity multiplier, and change your weight in 10-pound increments. Example 190 x 10 = 1900; 180 x 10 = 1800; 150 x 10 = 1500. As you will see, the more weight you lose, the less calories you need to support the weight. That's why, as you lose weight, the same calorie intake and activity level will lengthen the time it takes to lose weight. I'll explain that next.

_____ × _____ = _____
Weight   Activity Multiplier   Calories Required

_____ × _____ = _____
Weight   Activity Multiplier   Calories Required

_____ × _____ = _____
Weight   Activity Multiplier   Calories Required

How to lose weight using math!

To figure out how to lose weight in a healthy positive manner, first you have to figure out a healthy weight for your body type and height. There are nutrition calculators on the Internet that will help you figure this out. You can also find information at your local library, or call your doctor. For the nutrition calculator, I recommend you surf the Internet for several because I found one that had me as skin and bones! I hadn't weighed that amount since Jr. High. Take a few, and average them out.

Write your healthy weight here: _____

Write the activity multiplier you plan on doing (info given above) here: _____

Write your current intake of calories here: _____ To get your number, just keep track for a week, add them all up, and divide by 7.

To help in figuring out the formulas, I am going to use an example of a person that weighs 150 pounds and eats around 2000 calories a day. This person's weight should be 120 pounds and they've decided to exercise twice a week.

Write your numbers below to use in the formula.

Current Weight: _____

Current Calorie Intake: _____

Healthy Weight: _____

Activity Level: _____

First, you need to figure out how many calories your healthy body and activity level will require. 120 x 13.6 = 1632 calories

Write your calculation here:

_____ x _____ = _____
Healthy Weight   Activity Multiplier   Calories Required

Subtract your current calorie intake from your new goal, calorie intake.

2000 – 1632 = 368

_____ – _____ = _____
Current   Healthy   Difference

Okay. Now, how many days will it take you to lose 1 pound of body fat just by reducing calories?

There are 3500 calories in one pound of body fat

3500 divided by (calories per day less than you eat now) = Days to lose one pound.

3500/368 = 10 days to lose 1 pound

3500/_____ = _____
Difference from above   Days to lose one pound of body fat

DON'T BE DISCOURAGED BY THIS NUMBER! If you are lightweight and want to lose a small amount of weight (like 10 pounds), the days to lose one pound of body fat, increase! That's why it's so hard to lose the last 10 pounds. You can decrease this number with exercise—let me show you.

Adding exercise to your formula ...

What happens when you reduce your intake by 368 calories and add an activity to your routine? I will use "walking the dog for an hour" twice a week as my activity. Check out the Table of Activity in the back of the book. If your activity is not listed, get on the Internet and surf! It is usually listed with nutrition calculators. Or you can go to the library.

To do this equation, we are going to have to do some serious math. Okay? A scientific calculator isn't necessary though!

Because we are using "twice a week" as our added exercise, we are going to adjust our calculations for a week.

368 x 7 = 2576 calories reduced per week

352 x 2 = 704 extra calories burned per week

Use your numbers here:

_____ x 7 = _____ calories reduced per week
Calories Reduce

_____ x _____ = _____ extra burned per week
Activity   Days per week

Take your reduced calories (2576) + your extra calories burned (704) and add them together. 2576 + 704 = 3280 Now, divide that number by 7. 3280 divided by 7 days = 468 reduced calories per day.

_____ + _____ = _____ / 7 = _____
Reduced Calories Extra Calories Burned Total for the Week avg reduced per day

Using our "days to lose 1 pound calculation," let's figure out how many days to lose 1 pound of body fat.

3500/468 = 8 days

By walking the dog for an hour, twice a week, our example person will lose 1 pound of body fat every 8 days versus every 10 days. What if you add an average of 300 <u>extra</u> calories burned a day to the formula?

3500/(368+300=668) = 5 days to lose 1 pound of body fat.

If you exercise every day, do a calculation for yourself.

3500/ (_____ + _____ = _____) = _____
         Diff   Activity   Total   Days to lose 1 lb of body fat

<u>These formulas do not estimate water weight loss or gain.</u> We'll talk about that later in this section. If the weight loss appears to be slow to you, think of it like this: If you lose 1 pound of body fat every 7 days, in 6 months you will have lost 27 pounds of body fat. Now, go to the store and put 27 pounds of lard in a basket and push it around for an hour. Or stack 27 pounds of lard and measure it against your height. I think you'll find that 27 pounds of lard looks pretty close to an arm and a leg!

But wait … there's more to it!

<u>As you lose weight, you will need less calories to maintain that weight loss and more exercise.</u> In other words, you need to recalculate at each 10-pound loss to keep losing weight at your current rate. This is for both intake calories and calories burned. Remember the calculations you did above?

Let's take our example person and have them drop 10 pounds to 140. They are still keeping up the twice a week activity level.

140 lbs x 13.6 activity level = 1904

Goal is 120 lbs x 13.6 activity level = 1632

1904 – 1632 = 272 calories and 3500 (fat) divided by 272 calories = 13 days to lose 1 pound. Do you remember that, at 150 pounds, it only took 10 days to lose 1 pound with the intake at 1632? Now it will take 13 days.

Let's do your calculation, if you were to drop 10 pounds.

_____ X _____ = _____
Weight   Activity Multiplier   Calories Required for this weight

_____ X _____ = _____
Healthy Weight   Activity Multiplier   Calories Required for this weight

                        _____
                        Difference

3500/_____ = _____
      Difference   Days to lose 1 pound of body fat

If you check out the Table of Activity, you will notice that, as you lose weight, the amount of calories you burn also declines. Remember, our example person was walking the dog twice a week and burning 563 calories each time. At 140 pounds, our person is probably burning 500 calories doing this same exercise.

Why is it getting harder the lighter you get?? The body requires less food to maintain a lower weight and, since you are lighter, the body doesn't have to work as hard to burn calories. The best way to explain this is, to have you grab a five-pound weight and carry it for a few hours. After a while, it sure gets heavy. Once you get rid of the weight, it's a whole lot easier to move around. The same thing goes for your body. Lose 5 pounds, and it's a whole lot easier to manage, meaning you don't burn as many calories doing the same activity.

Water Weight

Water weight can be very misleading. Water weighs about 8.2 pounds per gallon. It is not unusual to retain considerable water when overweight. Most diets cause some degree of dehydration, with water loss greatly exceeding fat loss in the first week of the new diet. Therefore, the person who weighs daily will get an early psychological boost due to the water weight loss, only to be very disappointed, or even depressed, when this rapid weight loss slows or seems to stop in spite of continued heroic dietary and exercise efforts. Try to focus on the long term benefits and lifestyle changes, rather than the short term weight loss, and you will be much happier with your new self. (Water weight information provided to you by Dr. Brantley McNeel, MD.)

Whoa …. What does that mean?? If you are starting out on a diet plan to lose weight, you might lose a lot of water first and think your calculations from above are wrong! You may get really excited and think that every 3 days, you will lose 8 pounds. When you are back at the correct calculation (losing 1 pound every 5 days), you can become really disappointed and think your diet plan isn't working. That's why I put in the Progress Chart. You will be able to see your changes over a number of weeks and know that you are improving! Yeah!!! ☺

Remember in the diet instructions when I said you should drink a lot of water? Well, I talked with Dr. McNeel about this, and he gave me some more information to help us. If you intake water with a diet rich in sodium or salt, you will retain "salt water" which weighs even more than regular water. Who knew?? He went on to say that the best way to maintain a healthy "water supply" is to intake no more than 4 grams of salt a day. He also said the typical American diet averages around 20 grams of salt.

Remember that nutrition label? On there, it lists the amount of sodium the food contains. If you are having a problem retaining water, you might want to track your salt. How do you know if you are retaining water? Your fingers look swollen and you feel kind of bloated or full.

I've put some formula pages at two-week intervals. If you are using the advanced method, you can recalculate at these time frames.

So, what is the **Advanced Method**? Use your calculations to plan a strategy to control your weight gain or loss with your diet and exercise program.

To lose weight – Schedule your reduced calorie intake and increased exercise activity in advance. Using your calculations, you can estimate what your weight loss should be in a particular time frame and see if you are on track. Use the calorie intake line on the Diet Page to write down how many calories you will be intaking on that particular day. Add up how many calories you did intake, and write the difference in the Difference Block. You can use this number for your calculations and to track your progress towards your goal. Write the calories burned number you want to use for a particular day on the Calories Burned line on the Exercise Page. You can compare your activity with your goal.

What if I want to follow a particular diet plan? - Fill in your serving per week/day for that particular diet, like a vegetarian pyramid plan. For example, if the fruit servings are 3, the vegetable servings are 8, and the grains are 11, put those numbers in the appropriate food group block for however long you plan on pursuing this diet. This will help keep you informed of the requirements as you track and maintain your plan.

What if I want to plan for an athletic event? - Fill in the servings, calories required, and exercise goal for each week. By using the Progress Chart and the Exercise Pages, you will know if your plan is working. You can plan eight weeks in advance with the planner, and be able to concentrate on the athletic event.

Other perks on the Diet Page

I supplied a "Supplements" block for your use. It can be used to record any extra dietary supplements such as vitamins, herbs or product lines that you would like to use. I use this section to experiment. I take my measurements and baseline my diet. I then do the same exact routine, but add supplements or vitamins. I track it for two weeks and, by using my Progress Chart and Exercise Pages, I am able to see if I am wasting my money or if it is improving my performance. By the way, your body absorbs vitamins and minerals more efficiently when the intake comes in a food form versus a pill form. A "one a day" multi-vitamin is all a person really needs to maintain their health. What the body doesn't need, it flushes out. That is, unless you are overdosing. The body will, then, have side effects. Why spend money on extra vitamins when a good diet does the trick?

The "Mood and Complexion" block is to track how you are feeling and looking. When I am drinking all my water, eating a balanced diet, and exercising, I'm generally in a good mood and my skin clears up. Being hydrated and balanced also reduces the lines in my face. I haven't used a cream on the market that has had a more positive effect. Another plus point for healthy living!

It is also a good place to see if your supplements are changing your mood. I used a fat burner and found that it steadily made me more aggressive, broke out my skin (which made me depressed), and basically didn't change any of my "stats." Let's just say that family and co-workers clapped their hands when I decided to quit the fat burner phase of my diet experiment.

Daily Exercise Page

The daily exercise page tracks cardio, weight lifting, or at-home exercises. It also gives you a block to estimate how many calories you burned. This is great data when you are counting calories and using the formulas listed in the Diet Tips section.

To start using the page, write in the date. The calories burned line is used at the end of the exercising. You can estimate how many calories you burned by referring to the table at the back of the book. If you are exercising on a machine, the machine should calculate this amount for you. The next section is to record cardio time, distance, and strength training. I like to know how long I strength train so I can track how my supplements are performing, and use this time as part of my cardio workout.

The next table contains blocks for all the major muscle groups and some at-home exercises. Remember, some exercises don't use weights, so you won't have to fill in the weight block.

Easy Method

The simplest way to use this page is to write in the amount of time you spent doing cardio training and check off the muscle groups you worked or exercises you performed. It's that simple! In other words, if you did tricep exercises, check it off and move on to the next muscle group. As long as you work each muscle group, you will gain muscle tone.

Simple Method

Write in the amount of time and distance of your cardio training. If you strength trained, write in the amount of time you spent doing it, and if you had any increase in weight. (Example: 10 lbs on arms)

In the muscle group section, if you use the same weight and repetitions, write in the weight in the weight block and how many reps you performed.

Advanced Method

I get a little fancy on my weight workouts, so I use this method to track.

- If performing three sets at different weights and repetitions, I use slashes to record my weights (Example: 60/80/70), and my reps (e.g., 12/12/10).

- If I do several different exercises for the same muscle group, my weight and rep amounts usually stay the same. So, if I do two different tricep exercises, I write 30/40/30 in the weights and 24/24/20 in the repetitions.

- You can also "schedule" how many calories you are planning on burning for that particular day. For example: You calculate that you need to burn 1500 calories for the week. Look at the Table of Calories Burned chart and pick an activity to perform for each day. They should total 1500 calories for the week. Walk the dog one day, shoot baskets the next, go bowling, etc. It will keep your exercising different and your body won't get into a routine and stagnate. If you are working out with a partner, each one can choose a day of the week and surprise the other! Isn't this fun?

Blank blocks are for your use. Write in any exercise(s) you want to track. Remember, this is your book!

Exercise Instructions

If you need help with your exercises, here are some directions. You can also find pictures of the exercises on my web page, located at:

http://communities.msn.com/workoutnotebook

Push-ups: You will definitely develop all kinds of muscles doing this exercise. Remember not to do "butt-ups." Kneel down on the floor and walk your hands out until they are aligned with your shoulders. Make sure your hands have fingertips forward. Think of it as standing at a wall with your arms shoulder height and your hands flat against the wall. If you're like me, and weak in the push up department, cross your legs at the ankle and bend your legs up, resting on the top of your knees. "Top of the knee" does not mean "on the knee cap". So stretch further up with the hands to get off the cap. If you're a manly man, straighten out your legs and balance your body on your toes. As you go down, bend at your elbows, inhale, and touch your nose to the floor. You will work different muscle groups if you keep your elbows close to your body or bend them out to the side. You pick what you want to do. Now exhale on the way up, keeping your weight on the heal of your hands. Hold and squeeze those muscles, and release down, exhaling as you go. The best way to find out if you're doing push-ups correctly, is to do your sit-ups first. When you turn over to do your push-ups, if your abs aren't killing you, you are doing them incorrectly.

Sit-ups: There are many ways to do sit-ups.   To work your abdominal muscles during a usual sit-up, make sure you lift your shoulder blades off the floor, find a focal point on the ceiling to keep your chin off your chest, use your fingertips to hold your head, exhale as you come up, squeezing your belly button down into your body, and inhale on the way back down. I like to throw my legs up on the sofa. It helps to keep my lower back on the floor. Also, work in twisting to the left and right during sit-ups to work side abdominal muscles.

Lunges: This particular exercise is quite demanding. But once mastered, you'll notice a difference in your thighs and hamstrings. It requires perfect form, so get yourself in front of a mirror, and a chair for balance as you begin to master it. I start my lunges in the lower position first. Kneel down on one knee. Look in the mirror and make sure you have 90-degree angles with your legs. Your front knee should line up with your ankle. If it goes past that point, you will be hurting your knees and not working the thighs. Your body should be straight, like someone has tied a string to a point on top of your head and they're pulling it. Now raise yourself up, exhaling as you press off the heel of the front foot and on the toes of your back foot. Use the chair for balance if you need too. Squeeze at the top of the movement, release and inhale on the way back down. You can add hand weights, or a barbell resting on your shoulders, as you get better at this. Remember to change legs! You can also do this exercise by standing straight up and taking a long step forward with one leg, pushing back to the upright position, and then taking a long step forward with the other leg. Just remember that your knee never goes past your ankle.

Squats: This is another exercise that takes a little practice to master. This one can hurt your lower back and knees if done improperly. I mastered it using a chair at first.   Standing up, position your legs at shoulder distance. You can use either the inside or outside legs of the chair for a guide. I could feel the chair on the back of my legs. Now go prepare to sit in the chair, but stop as soon as you feel the edge of the seat on the back of your thighs. DO NOT sit in the chair! When you look down, your knees should not be over your toes. In this position, you should be pushing your butt back. Pretend someone has a string attached to your tailbone, and they're pulling it back. As you come back up to the standing position, squeeze your butt at the top of the movement, pushing your hips forward, and exhale. Your knees <u>do not</u> move in this exercise, and your weight is on the heel of your feet. Your knees act like a pivot point. To add arm movements, push your arms out during the down movement, and pull them in on the upward movement. To add weight, use a barbell that rests on your shoulders.

Lower Back: Lay on your belly with your hands, palms up, resting on the lower back. Keeping your toes touching the floor, raise your upper body so that your chest is off the floor. Exhale on the way up, squeeze the lower back muscles, release and inhale on the way down. As you get better, you can move your hands to your head, resting your fingertips on your ears, and do the same movement.

Diet Tips

My personal experience has been that I notice results of a new routine (good and bad) around the eight-week mark. While discussing this with a friend, he suggested that I take pictures every four weeks. I now see the changes and keep a positive attitude. I also notice where I am lacking, and I adjust my routine. So, break out the camera and get pictures of all the sides of your body. If your camera doesn't print the date, I suggest wearing a different outfit or hairstyle each time you take a photo.

The biggest mistake we make, is starving ourselves. The body needs a certain amount of calories to operate. If you deny the body the calories it needs, it will start a storing phase. If your body knows that food is being supplied on a consistent basis, it will have no problem releasing stored calories. Think of your body as a savings account. You put money into a savings account because you are either saving up for something, you think your cash flow may end, or because you have nothing else better to do with it. The body does the same thing with fat. It will start a storing phase because you've reduced your intake so low that it thinks the "food flow" is going to end, or because you yo-yo diet, causing it to think it may need some backup reserve to maintain bodily functions.

When you start your diet and exercise program, your body may be in one of these phases. My experience has been that the body needs around four weeks to switch phases. Why do you think it's so hard to lose weight after the New Year? From Thanksgiving to New Years is around six weeks, so your body gets all these extra calories and switches to the "I'm saving because I've got extra" phase. After the New Year, you start starving and exercising for one month. The body releases a little of the extra storage but, because it's starving, it switches to the "I'm saving for a rainy day" phase. You have to have a proper balance of intake and use to balance your body. This should be your ultimate goal.

Water weight - After having the water weight chat (see Diet Page Instructions—Advanced Method) with Dr. McNeel, I went back to my original book and noticed that when I began tracking my diet, I was bloated from all my water and, around the 4-week mark, it started to come off. Upon further investigation, I noticed that I had stopped doing the "workouts" at the vending machine, stopped eating so many chips and snacks at night, and quit drinking sodas. I had naturally reduced my sodium intake by staying away from pre-packaged food and those sodas!! This was another plus point for tracking my diet, and more proof that tracking your diet makes you naturally change your habits to healthy ones!

Eat six small meals a day instead of three. This is easier said than done, as it takes a lot of pre-planning if you work outside the home. But, it can work. I also found this to be the quickest way to let your body know you are feeding it on a consistent basis. <u>Make sure your proportions are smaller than your usual three-a-day meals, and stay within your calories requirement</u>. You can also use shakes and nutrition bars for the meals in between your three basics. Hey, who has time to think of what to eat six times a day?

Drink eight to ten cups of water a day. If you don't have time to go to the bathroom every twenty minutes, I suggest you stagger your water intake for your convenience. If you find yourself getting up in the middle of the night, it will last for about a week. I drink two cups in the morning, two cups at lunch, a cup when I get home, a cup during my workout, and a cup before I go to bed. During the day, I sip water at my desk. After a year of doing this, I no longer drink sodas at work. So, this habit turned out to have an economical benefit as well! Remember that salt intake, too. You don't want to add 8.2 pounds because you retained a gallon of water!

Reduce your alcohol consumption. A lot of people forget to track the martini after work or the six-pack during a football game. Alcohol calories do add up. This is also why I put it on the first lines of my calorie table. I don't want you to forget.

Keep "fat" snack foods that you can grab easily to a <u>minimum</u> in your home and at work. I don't buy cookies for one reason ~ I eat them, all of them, at one sitting. When my body craves a cookie, I go to the vending machine and buy a small package. This ends the craving, and I don't feel guilty. I also know a guy who keeps the mini-candy bars in his desk. It gets raided once a week! I also told him the kind I don't like, so he makes sure to buy those, too.

Reduce your trips to the vending machines at work. The hardest part of dieting is planning what you're going to eat when you're not at home. Don't get caught with the soda, chips, and candy-bar lunch.

Find a store that provides fresh fruit and vegetables. I shop at a discount store for groceries, but their inventory of fresh produce isn't the best. I now make my produce purchases elsewhere, and the produce has a longer shelf life.

When having food delivered to your home, try eating a salad before it arrives. When I do that, I don't attack the pizza delivery person at the door. The salad has had time to fill me up, and I eat only two slices instead of the usual six!

Keep fresh deli meats, and those little tiny vegetables, in bags in the fridge at all times. When I'm scrounging around in there, I just open the bag, take out a few pieces, and munch.

Beware of dried or too much fruit. Dried fruit is good for your fruit group, but it isn't as filling as fresh. Fruits contain sugar instead of fat, so, if you eat a lot of fruit, you may intake a lot of sugar. The body will burn the sugars first before they start on fat storage. Also, don't eat too many dried fruits at one time, or you'll be spending a lot of time in the bathroom. I did lose a few pounds, though.

It really doesn't make a difference if you eat in the morning or late at night. Calories are calories. If you require 1200, it doesn't matter when you eat them. I prefer to eat late in the evening. When I want to fool my body into thinking I'm eating in the morning, I have a protein-carb shake before I leave the house. It's quick and easy. I usually make it a double, and take some to work. The point is, to intake consistently every day. If your body knows for four weeks that you are going to feed it late at night, it will adjust its use.

The best diet tip I know is to have fun experimenting with your diet and body. You've got all the time in the world. Using **The Workout Notebook** has taught me a lot about what I can do with it! If you think of your diet as a game, and be patient, you will discover good health and a new image.

Attitude Tips

If you've never been successful with a diet plan, it's probably because you were trying a crazy fad diet, or you gave up before your body could produce results. Be Patient ~ remember those calculations.

When you begin a new program, tell yourself that your body is a work of art, and you are developing a masterpiece. Developing a masterpiece takes time. Hey, I'm pretty sure di Vinci took more than a few weeks to paint the Mona Lisa.

When setting your goals, be realistic so you don't set yourself up for failure. I said in the introduction, "How can you fail from where you begin?" What that means is, track what you're doing now, establish a baseline, and improve. How can you fail? For example, if you don't drink water, and now you are drinking one cup a day, you've improved! Use these small goals to keep yourself motivated.

Be realistic when planning your ultimate goal. I want to look like the women in lingerie magazines but, in reality, diet and exercise won't make me taller or twenty years old again! Look at your canvas and paint YOUR picture. My goal is to develop intake and expending habits so I no longer have to track! Okay, I want to look good in shorts, too!

Did I say "Be Patient??" Be patient with yourself. If you have a bad diet or exercise day, tomorrow you can start again. Just make sure you start! Many times I've said, "I'll just skip today," and it ends up being two months, and I am back at my beginning.

Try to find yourself a support friend or group because you will need it. I hate to say this, but when you start a new routine, your significant other or family will end their support at about week three. Your changes affect them, and no one voices their dislikes more than your loved ones. If you don't give in, around week eight they will have adjusted their routine to yours, and have found other things to complain about.

Keep an independent focused attitude, and you won't cave in. You will have people in your life that, though they love you, they will make fun of your exercising and dieting. They will offer you foods that you are avoiding, offer you alcoholic beverages when you are cutting back, and discourage your workouts. Do not let these people make you feel guilty about taking care of yourself. In reality, they know they should be doing the same thing!

The best attitude tip I have, is to be a little selfish for a few months. Don't let other's guilt-trips keep you from being healthy and your best. I guarantee that people will notice the "new you" in your attitude, your compassion, your quality of work, and in the way you carry yourself. You will get compliments from people who never gave you the time of day. When I am on track, I gain an inch in height due to good posture. It's called self-confidence. It will have a ripple effect on everything and everyone in your life.

Exercise Tips

If you're new to exercising, remember not to shock your body. Start out increasing your activity slowly. What do I mean by "shock your body?" If you are a sedentary person (you haven't increased your heart rate in years), the blood vessels in your body have not been flexed. When you exercise, you increase the blood flow through your vessels, which stretches the vessel walls, making them pliable. Unexercised vessels are stiff. If you start your exercise program with a one-mile run or spinning class, for instance, the blood flow will increase at a tremendous rate through those vessels. They haven't been stretched in years. so they cramp, tighten, and stress out! You feel like you're having a heart attack. Your blood vessels feel like they're having a heart attack! Be careful out there when you're new to exercising.

Your body needs to rest. Make sure you take some time off of exercising to let it heal. You also need to get eight hours of rest to let the muscles rebuild, so hit the sack at night.

What should I do?

If you want to start an exercise program, you can join a gym or start at home. Below are some at home exercising ideas, and then suggestions on how to get started.

Exercise Ideas: Push-ups, sit-ups, lunges, squats, lower back, pull-ups, bicep curls, triceps, arm-lifting movements with weights. Instructions for these ideas are listed at the end of this section.

Cardio Ideas: Run in place, jumping jacks, dance and twist, make a step and go up and down on it. Just do something to elevate your heart rate. The goal is to be able to do it steadily for 20 minutes, 3 to 4 times a week. Remember the goal is 20 minutes. Don't do that your very first day!

To begin your program, I suggest starting with a cardio workout. Plan to do this activity for 5 to 10 minutes for the first week, then increase your time each week until you reach your goal.

To start a cardio activity

- Stretch for warm-up
- Perform 5-10 minutes of activity
- Stretch to cool down.

I suggest that when you begin your exercise activity, that you plan to do stretching exercises first. This will minimize any muscle discomfort as you begin. On the second day, add more repetitions and some new exercises. Build yourself up slowly until you reach your goal.

Stretching exercises can be as easy as touching your toes, and then reaching to the ceiling and slightly reaching your arms back over your head.

To start an exercise activity

- Stretch and jump around a little bit to loosen up

- Do three sets of 8 repetitions of each exercise

- Cool down with stretching.

Other ideas to help you with your new program are:

- Keep a glass of water or water bottle nearby.

- If you have family members around the house, tell them to bug off while you're working out. My kids have a tendency to "need to talk to me" during my workouts at home. I lock the door, crank up the music, and hope they don't burn down the house. If you're not so brave, find a way to include them. Working out looks like fun. And it is!

- Try to have a full-length mirror near your workout area. If you are using weights or mastering an exercise, you'll need to watch yourself for proper form.

- If you want to add weights to your at-home workout, and the budget says, "I don't think so," use cans of food, or fill empty plastic milk containers with water.

- Here's the best tip about working out at home ~ do it in your underwear! Really.... It's great, and you don't have to worry about a clothing expense.

If you are interested in adding equipment to your workout, I started with two 2-pounds hand weights, and made purchases as I got stronger. I have a set of 2lb, 5lb, 8lb and 10lb hand weights. After the 10lb purchase, as I increased, I put two weights together, such as the 10lb and the 2lb for bicep curls. Expect to pay $1.00 per pound at most sporting stores. I also have a set of 5lb ankle weights.

What should I do? I've just joined the gym?

- Take a towel with you. The towel is for you to use while working out on the equipment. I hate to put my face on anything that 500 other people have used. Also, use the towel to wipe off your sweat when you're done. Other patrons will look upon you with disgust if you leave the equipment wet.

- Take a water bottle with you. Sip water during your workout. Muscles work better when they are hydrated, and you can count it towards your 8 cups a day.

- Dress comfortably. I like to wear a tight pair of shorts because, when you workout on some machines, people can see right up loose shorts. Most gyms have mirrors, and you don't want to shock yourself or other people.

- Make sure you have an employee of the gym show you how to use all the equipment properly. You are the customer. I don't know about you, but I work hard for my money, and so should they! Most gyms give you a free training session, so make sure to ask for one.

- You are ready to start working out. Hey, don't forget to warm up first! On weight training days, I use a treadmill or bike for five minutes to get the blood pumping. Then I do some basic stretching like we learned in school. For cardio days, I stretch first, and then warm up on the equipment for five minutes before I start my workout.

- When using the cardio machines, don't quit because you can't figure out the machine. Ask someone for help. It also takes some time to get the movements down. I ordered a NordicTrack and it took me 3 weeks to figure out how to add my arms to the movement.

- When using weights, don't be macho-man your first time out. Practice your form first, and then increase your weight. And don't lift like a bat out of hell either! The best way to get the full benefit from lifting weights is to lift, squeeze, and release. I use those words to help me focus. So, remember—lift, squeeze, release.

- Practice good breathing! Exhale on the "lift" movement, inhale on the release. You will start the exercise in the released position.

- Use the mirrors. If you are not using proper form, especially with the free weights (weights not connected to a machine), you will hurt yourself, you won't get the full-benefit of the exercise, and no one at the gym will think you're vain. Unless of course, you are doing your hair or make-up!

- If you need to use a machine, and someone is just sitting on it, ask to work in your sets. The gym has rules of etiquette. Sharing the machines is one of them. On the same token, if someone asks to work in with you, please oblige.

- If you forget how to use a machine, watch the person who's using it before you. Your best bet, though, is to ask someone. I have never experienced a person in the gym not wanting to help me. But, don't ask someone when they are doing their sets!

- Don't be a chatterbox. Most people want to get in and out of the gym as quickly as possible. I like going to the gym because it's the only time during the day that I don't have to talk.

- Don't do too much, too soon! One 8-rep exercise per muscle group with a light weight is plenty. I once saw a new guy take a spinning class, then attend a circuit training class. He never returned to the gym. I'm still wondering if he ever made it out of bed!

- It's the day after your new workout and you can't get out of bed! This is NORMAL!!! And guess what? Tomorrow will be even worse! But, make sure you go back to the gym in two days, even if you can't lift your arm to scratch your head. I take a three-day break after the second session, and my body is ready to take on the world. You will never be that sore again if you stay with your program.

What should I do? I just joined a class?

- Take a towel and a bottle of water.

- Get to the class early so you can set up your equipment. The class will start without you, and you won't want to miss the warm-up. This is also a great time to talk with the instructor. The instructor is hired by the gym to serve you. Remember, you are the customer. Try to position yourself close to the instructor during the class. The instructor can guide you on form during the workout. Once you're good at it, you can sneak to the back.

- You get stuck next to the Amazon body in a thong! Don't freak out or feel bad about yourself. Use this person during the workout. This person generally has a lot of positive energy, and you can watch how they do the movements. I measure my progress against this person. If I can keep up with the Amazon, I know I'm getting better!

- It's the day after your new class, and you can't get out of bed! Same rules as above. Go to the next scheduled class and take a three-day break. You'll be back on track. Really!

The best tip I have for any type of exercise routine is, be sure to DO IT! When your body is weak, lighten up on the amount of weight you use. If your legs are tired, walk instead of running. If I miss a day because of "life in general," either I make up the one I missed along with my usual workout the next day or I consider it my "rest day". Make sure you have plenty of these. Why? The muscle develops during the rest phase, not during the workout. The workout tears down the muscle. It is through rest that it builds and grows. I know a guy who works out every day of the week. I've yet to see any real improvement in his body, and he looks tired. Another case of "too much of a good thing isn't good for you." If you are clueless as to what you want to do, use the Table of Activity, and try a few things! You'll find something that you like.

Tracking Pages

This section is set up for daily diet and exercise tracking. I have divided it into one-week sections for your convenience. Each section will have 7 days of tracking. You can use this several ways. You can be gung-ho and complete all the weeks in one try or, if life gets in your way, you can begin where you stopped.

Tracking Pages
Week One

Did you ...

- Write your measurements on the Progress Chart?

- Decide how you are going to track your diet?

- Plan a simple menu and go grocery shopping?

- Decide how you are going to exercise?

- Take pictures of yourself?

If you answered "yes" to all of the above, let's get started!

Diet Page - Week One - Day 1

Calorie Intake Required: _____   Date: _____

Fruits (2-4 Servings)				**Servings Per Week/Day:**			
1 piece, 1/2 cup canned, 1 oz dried, 6 oz juice				**Fat Calories**			
						Total	

Vegetables (3-5 Servings)				**Servings Per Week/Day:**			
1 piece, 1 cup raw, 1/2 cup canned, 1 oz dried, 6 oz juice						**Fat**	
						Total	

Whole Grains (6-11 servings)				**Servings Per Week/Day:**			
1 slice bread, 1/2 muffin/bun/bagel/tortilla, 1/2 c. pasta/rice, 1oz b/fast cereal						**Fat**	
						Total	

Meats, Beans, Eggs (2-3 Servings)				**Servings Per Week/Day:**			
1 egg, 3 oz of meat/fish/poultry, 15 nuts, 1 cup beans						**Fat**	
						Total	

Dairy Products (2-3 servings)				**Servings Per Week/Day:**			
1 cup milk, 1 oz cheese, 1 cup yogurt						**Fat**	
						Total	

Fats, Oil, Butters (Sparingly)				**Servings Per Week/Day:**			
1 Tbsp for oils, dressings, mayo, nut butters and butter/margarine						**Fat**	
						Total	

Sweets & Snacks (Sparingly)				**Servings Per Week/Day:**			
1 piece of candy, 1 serving of fast food, 1 serving of snack foods						**Fat**	
						Total	

Beverages/Water (8-10 cups)				**Servings Per Week/Day:**			
1 cup of water (Track your soda, coffee, tea, & alcohol calories here)							
						Total	

Difference: _____   Total Calories: _____

Supplements

Mood and Complexion

Mood		Complexion	
Notes:			

Exercise Page - Week One - Day 1

Date: _____   Calories Burned: _____

Remember to warm up prior to exercising!

Cardio Training			Strength Training	
Time	Distance	Cal Burn	Time	Increases

Muscle Group	Weight	Repetitions
Upper Body Exercises		
Neck		
Delts (upper arm)		
Traps (Upper back)		
Pecs (chest)		
Biceps (front arm)		
Triceps (back arm)		
Oblique (waist)		
Abs (stomach)		
Lats (middle back)		
Lower Body Exercises		
Lower Back		
Inner Thigh		
Outer Thigh		
Quads (front thigh)		
Gluts (buttocks)		
Hamstring (back thigh)		
Calves (lower back leg)		
Push-ups		
Sit-ups		
Lunges		
Squats		

Diet Page - Week One - Day 2

Calorie Intake Required: _____   Date: _____

Fruits (2-4 Servings)						Servings Per Week/Day:		
1 piece, 1/2 cup canned, 1 oz dried, 6 oz juice						Fat Calories		
							Total	

Vegetables (3-5 Servings)						Servings Per Week/Day:		
1 piece, 1 cup raw, 1/2 cup canned, 1 oz dried, 6 oz juice							Fat	
							Total	

Whole Grains (6-11 servings)						Servings Per Week/Day:		
1 slice bread, 1/2 muffin/bun/bagel/tortilla, 1/2 c. pasta/rice, 1oz b/fast cereal							Fat	
							Total	

Meats, Beans, Eggs (2-3 Servings)						Servings Per Week/Day:		
1 egg, 3 oz of meat/fish/poultry, 15 nuts, 1 cup beans							Fat	
							Total	

Dairy Products (2-3 servings)						Servings Per Week/Day:		
1 cup milk, 1 oz cheese, 1 cup yogurt							Fat	
							Total	

Fats, Oil, Butters (Sparingly)						Servings Per Week/Day:		
1 Tbsp for oils, dressings, mayo, nut butters and butter/margarine							Fat	
							Total	

Sweets & Snacks (Sparingly)						Servings Per Week/Day:		
1 piece of candy, 1 serving of fast food, 1 serving of snack foods							Fat	
							Total	

Beverages/Water (8-10 cups)						Servings Per Week/Day:		
1 cup of water (Track your soda, coffee, tea, & alcohol calories here)								
							Total	

Difference: _____   Total Calories: _____

Supplements

Mood and Complexion

Mood		Complexion	
Notes:			

Exercise Page - Week One - Day 2

Date: _____   Calories Burned: _____

Remember to warm up prior to exercising!

Cardio Training			Strength Training	
Time	Distance	Cal Burn	Time	Increases

Muscle Group	Weight	Repetitions
Upper Body Exercises		
Neck		
Delts (upper arm)		
Traps (Upper back)		
Pecs (chest)		
Biceps (front arm)		
Triceps (back arm)		
Oblique (waist)		
Abs (stomach)		
Lats (middle back)		
Lower Body Exercises		
Lower Back		
Inner Thigh		
Outer Thigh		
Quads (front thigh)		
Gluts (buttocks)		
Hamstring (back thigh)		
Calves (lower back leg)		
Push-ups		
Sit-ups		
Lunges		
Squats		

Diet Page - Week One - Day 3

Calorie Intake Required: _____   Date: _____

Fruits (2-4 Servings)					Servings Per Week/Day:			
1 piece, 1/2 cup canned, 1 oz dried, 6 oz juice					Fat Calories			
							Total	

Vegetables (3-5 Servings)					Servings Per Week/Day:			
1 piece, 1 cup raw, 1/2 cup canned, 1 oz dried, 6 oz juice							Fat	
							Total	

Whole Grains (6-11 servings)					Servings Per Week/Day:			
1 slice bread, 1/2 muffin/bun/bagel/tortilla, 1/2 c. pasta/rice, 1oz b/fast cereal							Fat	
							Total	

Meats, Beans, Eggs (2-3 Servings)					Servings Per Week/Day:			
1 egg, 3 oz of meat/fish/poultry, 15 nuts, 1 cup beans							Fat	
							Total	

Dairy Products (2-3 servings)					Servings Per Week/Day:			
1 cup milk, 1 oz cheese, 1 cup yogurt							Fat	
							Total	

Fats, Oil, Butters (Sparingly)					Servings Per Week/Day:			
1 Tbsp for oils, dressings, mayo, nut butters and butter/margarine							Fat	
							Total	

Sweets & Snacks (Sparingly)					Servings Per Week/Day:			
1 piece of candy, 1 serving of fast food, 1 serving of snack foods							Fat	
							Total	

Beverages/Water (8-10 cups)					Servings Per Week/Day:			
1 cup of water (Track your soda, coffee, tea, & alcohol calories here)								
							Total	

Difference: _____   Total Calories: _____

Supplements

Mood and Complexion

Mood		Complexion	
Notes:			

Exercise Page - Week One - Day 3

Date: _____   Calories Burned: _____

Remember to warm up prior to exercising!

Cardio Training			Strength Training	
Time	Distance	Cal Burn	Time	Increases

Muscle Group	Weight	Repetitions
Upper Body Exercises		
Neck		
Delts (upper arm)		
Traps (Upper back)		
Pecs (chest)		
Biceps (front arm)		
Triceps (back arm)		
Oblique (waist)		
Abs (stomach)		
Lats (middle back)		
Lower Body Exercises		
Lower Back		
Inner Thigh		
Outer Thigh		
Quads (front thigh)		
Gluts (buttocks)		
Hamstring (back thigh)		
Calves (lower back leg)		
Push-ups		
Sit-ups		
Lunges		
Squats		

Diet Page - Week One - Day 4

Calorie Intake Required: _____   Date: _____

Fruits (2-4 Servings)					Servings Per Week/Day:			
1 piece, 1/2 cup canned, 1 oz dried, 6 oz juice					Fat Calories			
							Total	

Vegetables (3-5 Servings)					Servings Per Week/Day:			
1 piece, 1 cup raw, 1/2 cup canned, 1 oz dried, 6 oz juice						Fat		
							Total	

Whole Grains (6-11 servings)					Servings Per Week/Day:			
1 slice bread, 1/2 muffin/bun/bagel/tortilla, 1/2 c. pasta/rice, 1oz b/fast cereal						Fat		
							Total	

Meats, Beans, Eggs (2-3 Servings)					Servings Per Week/Day:			
1 egg, 3 oz of meat/fish/poultry, 15 nuts, 1 cup beans						Fat		
							Total	

Dairy Products (2-3 servings)					Servings Per Week/Day:			
1 cup milk, 1 oz cheese, 1 cup yogurt						Fat		
							Total	

Fats, Oil, Butters (Sparingly)					Servings Per Week/Day:			
1 Tbsp for oils, dressings, mayo, nut butters and butter/margarine						Fat		
							Total	

Sweets & Snacks (Sparingly)					Servings Per Week/Day:			
1 piece of candy, 1 serving of fast food, 1 serving of snack foods						Fat		
							Total	

Beverages/Water (8-10 cups)					Servings Per Week/Day:			
1 cup of water (Track your soda, coffee, tea, & alcohol calories here)								
							Total	

Difference: _____   Total Calories: _____

Supplements

Mood and Complexion

Mood		Complexion	
Notes:			

Exercise Page - Week One - Day 4

Date: _____   Calories Burned: _____

Remember to warm up prior to exercising!

Cardio Training			Strength Training	
Time	Distance	Cal Burn	Time	Increases

Muscle Group	Weight	Repetitions
Upper Body Exercises		
Neck		
Delts (upper arm)		
Traps (Upper back)		
Pecs (chest)		
Biceps (front arm)		
Triceps (back arm)		
Oblique (waist)		
Abs (stomach)		
Lats (middle back)		
Lower Body Exercises		
Lower Back		
Inner Thigh		
Outer Thigh		
Quads (front thigh)		
Gluts (buttocks)		
Hamstring (back thigh)		
Calves (lower back leg)		
Push-ups		
Sit-ups		
Lunges		
Squats		

Diet Page - Week One - Day 5

Calorie Intake Required: _____   Date: _____

Fruits (2-4 Servings)						Servings Per Week/Day:			
1 piece, 1/2 cup canned, 1 oz dried, 6 oz juice						Fat Calories			
								Total	

Vegetables (3-5 Servings)						Servings Per Week/Day:			
1 piece, 1 cup raw, 1/2 cup canned, 1 oz dried, 6 oz juice								Fat	
								Total	

Whole Grains (6-11 servings)						Servings Per Week/Day:			
1 slice bread, 1/2 muffin/bun/bagel/tortilla, 1/2 c. pasta/rice, 1oz b/fast cereal								Fat	
								Total	

Meats, Beans, Eggs (2-3 Servings)						Servings Per Week/Day:			
1 egg, 3 oz of meat/fish/poultry, 15 nuts, 1 cup beans								Fat	
								Total	

Dairy Products (2-3 servings)						Servings Per Week/Day:			
1 cup milk, 1 oz cheese, 1 cup yogurt								Fat	
								Total	

Fats, Oil, Butters (Sparingly)						Servings Per Week/Day:			
1 Tbsp for oils, dressings, mayo, nut butters and butter/margarine								Fat	
								Total	

Sweets & Snacks (Sparingly)						Servings Per Week/Day:			
1 piece of candy, 1 serving of fast food, 1 serving of snack foods								Fat	
								Total	

Beverages/Water (8-10 cups)						Servings Per Week/Day:			
1 cup of water (Track your soda, coffee, tea, & alcohol calories here)									
								Total	

Difference: _____   Total Calories: _____

Supplements

Mood and Complexion

Mood		Complexion	
Notes:			

Exercise Page - Week One - Day 5

Date: _____   Calories Burned: _____

Remember to warm up prior to exercising!

Cardio Training			Strength Training	
Time	Distance	Cal Burn	Time	Increases

Muscle Group	Weight	Repetitions
Upper Body Exercises		
Neck		
Delts (upper arm)		
Traps (Upper back)		
Pecs (chest)		
Biceps (front arm)		
Triceps (back arm)		
Oblique (waist)		
Abs (stomach)		
Lats (middle back)		
Lower Body Exercises		
Lower Back		
Inner Thigh		
Outer Thigh		
Quads (front thigh)		
Gluts (buttocks)		
Hamstring (back thigh)		
Calves (lower back leg)		
Push-ups		
Sit-ups		
Lunges		
Squats		

Diet Page - Week One - Day 6

Calorie Intake Required: _____   Date: _____

Fruits (2-4 Servings)					Servings Per Week/Day:			
1 piece, 1/2 cup canned, 1 oz dried, 6 oz juice					Fat Calories			
							Total	

Vegetables (3-5 Servings)					Servings Per Week/Day:			
1 piece, 1 cup raw, 1/2 cup canned, 1 oz dried, 6 oz juice							Fat	
							Total	

Whole Grains (6-11 servings)					Servings Per Week/Day:			
1 slice bread, 1/2 muffin/bun/bagel/tortilla, 1/2 c. pasta/rice, 1oz b/fast cereal							Fat	
							Total	

Meats, Beans, Eggs (2-3 Servings)					Servings Per Week/Day:			
1 egg, 3 oz of meat/fish/poultry, 15 nuts, 1 cup beans							Fat	
							Total	

Dairy Products (2-3 servings)					Servings Per Week/Day:			
1 cup milk, 1 oz cheese, 1 cup yogurt							Fat	
							Total	

Fats, Oil, Butters (Sparingly)					Servings Per Week/Day:			
1 Tbsp for oils, dressings, mayo, nut butters and butter/margarine							Fat	
							Total	

Sweets & Snacks (Sparingly)					Servings Per Week/Day:			
1 piece of candy, 1 serving of fast food, 1 serving of snack foods							Fat	
							Total	

Beverages/Water (8-10 cups)					Servings Per Week/Day:			
1 cup of water (Track your soda, coffee, tea, & alcohol calories here)								
							Total	

Difference: _____   Total Calories: _____

Supplements

Mood and Complexion

Mood		Complexion	
Notes:			

Exercise Page - Week One - Day 6

Date: _____   Calories Burned: _____

Remember to warm up prior to exercising!

Cardio Training			Strength Training	
Time	Distance	Cal Burn	Time	Increases

Muscle Group	Weight	Repetitions
Upper Body Exercises		
Neck		
Delts (upper arm)		
Traps (Upper back)		
Pecs (chest)		
Biceps (front arm)		
Triceps (back arm)		
Oblique (waist)		
Abs (stomach)		
Lats (middle back)		
Lower Body Exercises		
Lower Back		
Inner Thigh		
Outer Thigh		
Quads (front thigh)		
Gluts (buttocks)		
Hamstring (back thigh)		
Calves (lower back leg)		
Push-ups		
Sit-ups		
Lunges		
Squats		

Diet Page - Week One - Day 7

Calorie Intake Required: _____   Date: _____

Fruits (2-4 Servings)						Servings Per Week/Day:		
1 piece, 1/2 cup canned, 1 oz dried, 6 oz juice						Fat Calories		
							Total	

Vegetables (3-5 Servings)						Servings Per Week/Day:		
1 piece, 1 cup raw, 1/2 cup canned, 1 oz dried, 6 oz juice							Fat	
							Total	

Whole Grains (6-11 servings)						Servings Per Week/Day:		
1 slice bread, 1/2 muffin/bun/bagel/tortilla, 1/2 c. pasta/rice, 1oz b/fast cereal							Fat	
							Total	

Meats,Beans, Eggs (2-3 Servings)						Servings Per Week/Day:		
1 egg, 3 oz of meat/fish/poultry, 15 nuts, 1 cup beans							Fat	
							Total	

Dairy Products (2-3 servings)						Servings Per Week/Day:		
1 cup milk, 1 oz cheese, 1 cup yogurt							Fat	
							Total	

Fats, Oil, Butters (Sparingly)						Servings Per Week/Day:		
1 Tbsp for oils, dressings, mayo, nut butters and butter/margarine							Fat	
							Total	

Sweets & Snacks (Sparingly)						Servings Per Week/Day:		
1 piece of candy, 1 serving of fast food, 1 serving of snack foods							Fat	
							Total	

Beverages/Water (8-10 cups)						Servings Per Week/Day:		
1 cup of water (Track your soda, coffee, tea, & alcohol calories here)								
							Total	

Difference: _____   Total Calories: _____

Supplements

Mood and Complexion

Mood		Complexion	
Notes:			

Exercise Page - Week One - Day 7

Date: _____   Calories Burned: _____

Remember to warm up prior to exercising!

Cardio Training			Strength Training	
Time	Distance	Cal Burn	Time	Increases

Muscle Group	Weight	Repetitions
Upper Body Exercises		
Neck		
Delts (upper arm)		
Traps (Upper back)		
Pecs (chest)		
Biceps (front arm)		
Triceps (back arm)		
Oblique (waist)		
Abs (stomach)		
Lats (middle back)		
Lower Body Exercises		
Lower Back		
Inner Thigh		
Outer Thigh		
Quads (front thigh)		
Gluts (buttocks)		
Hamstring (back thigh)		
Calves (lower back leg)		
Push-ups		
Sit-ups		
Lunges		
Squats		

Notes:
Add your calories for the week on this table.

Day Of Week	Intake Calories	Burned Calories
Sunday		
Monday		
Tuesday		
Wednesday		
Thursday		
Friday		
Saturday		
Totals		

Tracking Pages
Week Two

Did you ...

- Write your measurements on the Progress Chart?

- Get the hang of tracking your diet & exercise?

- Go grocery shopping?

- Make adjustments to your routine by just looking at your diet?

Remember ...

- Your body is still in its "former" phase, so don't be disappointed if your measurements have increased (like your weight). You may have been in a starving phase and your body is storing up all that good food. I gained three pounds my first week, and had to break out my "fat" pants. You may also be gaining some water weight from your 8 to 10 cups of water. Remember to watch your sodium or salt intake.

- If you changed your eating habits immediately, hopefully you noticed something positive! Write it down here.

Diet Page - Week Two - Day 1

Calorie Intake Required: _____   Date: _____

Fruits (2-4 Servings)							Servings Per Week/Day:	
1 piece, 1/2 cup canned, 1 oz dried, 6 oz juice							Fat Calories	
							Total	

Vegetables (3-5 Servings)							Servings Per Week/Day:	
1 piece, 1 cup raw, 1/2 cup canned, 1 oz dried, 6 oz juice							Fat	
							Total	

Whole Grains (6-11 servings)							Servings Per Week/Day:	
1 slice bread, 1/2 muffin/bun/bagel/tortilla, 1/2 c. pasta/rice, 1oz b/fast cereal							Fat	
							Total	

Meats, Beans, Eggs (2-3 Servings)							Servings Per Week/Day:	
1 egg, 3 oz of meat/fish/poultry, 15 nuts, 1 cup beans							Fat	
							Total	

Dairy Products (2-3 servings)							Servings Per Week/Day:	
1 cup milk, 1 oz cheese, 1 cup yogurt							Fat	
							Total	

Fats, Oil, Butters (Sparingly)							Servings Per Week/Day:	
1 Tbsp for oils, dressings, mayo, nut butters and butter/margarine							Fat	
							Total	

Sweets & Snacks (Sparingly)							Servings Per Week/Day:	
1 piece of candy, 1 serving of fast food, 1 serving of snack foods							Fat	
							Total	

Beverages/Water (8-10 cups)							Servings Per Week/Day:	
1 cup of water (Track your soda, coffee, tea, & alcohol calories here)								
							Total	

Difference: _____   Total Calories: _____

Supplements

Mood and Complexion

Mood		Complexion	
Notes:			

Exercise Page - Week Two - Day 1
Date: _____   Calories Burned: _____

Remember to warm up prior to exercising!

Cardio Training			Strength Training	
Time	Distance	Cal Burn	Time	Increases

Muscle Group	Weight	Repetitions
Upper Body Exercises		
Neck		
Delts (upper arm)		
Traps (Upper back)		
Pecs (chest)		
Biceps (front arm)		
Triceps (back arm)		
Oblique (waist)		
Abs (stomach)		
Lats (middle back)		
Lower Body Exercises		
Lower Back		
Inner Thigh		
Outer Thigh		
Quads (front thigh)		
Gluts (buttocks)		
Hamstring (back thigh)		
Calves (lower back leg)		
Push-ups		
Sit-ups		
Lunges		
Squats		

Diet Page - Week Two - Day 2

Calorie Intake Required: _____   Date: _____

Fruits (2-4 Servings)						Servings Per Week/Day:		
1 piece, 1/2 cup canned, 1 oz dried, 6 oz juice						Fat Calories		
							Total	

Vegetables (3-5 Servings)						Servings Per Week/Day:		
1 piece, 1 cup raw, 1/2 cup canned, 1 oz dried, 6 oz juice							Fat	
							Total	

Whole Grains (6-11 servings)						Servings Per Week/Day:		
1 slice bread, 1/2 muffin/bun/bagel/tortilla, 1/2 c. pasta/rice, 1oz b/fast cereal							Fat	
							Total	

Meats, Beans, Eggs (2-3 Servings)						Servings Per Week/Day:		
1 egg, 3 oz of meat/fish/poultry, 15 nuts, 1 cup beans							Fat	
							Total	

Dairy Products (2-3 servings)						Servings Per Week/Day:		
1 cup milk, 1 oz cheese, 1 cup yogurt							Fat	
							Total	

Fats, Oil, Butters (Sparingly)						Servings Per Week/Day:		
1 Tbsp for oils, dressings, mayo, nut butters and butter/margarine							Fat	
							Total	

Sweets & Snacks (Sparingly)						Servings Per Week/Day:		
1 piece of candy, 1 serving of fast food, 1 serving of snack foods							Fat	
							Total	

Beverages/Water (8-10 cups)						Servings Per Week/Day:		
1 cup of water (Track your soda, coffee, tea, & alcohol calories here)								
							Total	

Difference: _____   Total Calories: _____

Supplements

Mood and Complexion

Mood		Complexion	
Notes:			

Exercise Page - Week Two - Day 2

Date: _____   Calories Burned: _____

Remember to warm up prior to exercising!

Cardio Training			Strength Training	
Time	Distance	Cal Burn	Time	Increases

Muscle Group	Weight	Repetitions
Upper Body Exercises		
Neck		
Delts (upper arm)		
Traps (Upper back)		
Pecs (chest)		
Biceps (front arm)		
Triceps (back arm)		
Oblique (waist)		
Abs (stomach)		
Lats (middle back)		
Lower Body Exercises		
Lower Back		
Inner Thigh		
Outer Thigh		
Quads (front thigh)		
Gluts (buttocks)		
Hamstring (back thigh)		
Calves (lower back leg)		
Push-ups		
Sit-ups		
Lunges		
Squats		

Diet Page - Week Two - Day 3

Calorie Intake Required: _____   Date: _____

Fruits (2-4 Servings)					**Servings Per Week/Day:**			
1 piece, 1/2 cup canned, 1 oz dried, 6 oz juice					**Fat Calories**			
							Total	

Vegetables (3-5 Servings)					**Servings Per Week/Day:**			
1 piece, 1 cup raw, 1/2 cup canned, 1 oz dried, 6 oz juice					**Fat**			
							Total	

Whole Grains (6-11 servings)					**Servings Per Week/Day:**			
1 slice bread, 1/2 muffin/bun/bagel/tortilla, 1/2 c. pasta/rice, 1oz b/fast cereal					**Fat**			
							Total	

Meats,Beans, Eggs (2-3 Servings)					**Servings Per Week/Day:**			
1 egg, 3 oz of meat/fish/poultry, 15 nuts, 1 cup beans					**Fat**			
							Total	

Dairy Products (2-3 servings)					**Servings Per Week/Day:**			
1 cup milk, 1 oz cheese, 1 cup yogurt					**Fat**			
							Total	

Fats, Oil, Butters (Sparingly)					**Servings Per Week/Day:**			
1 Tbsp for oils, dressings, mayo, nut butters and butter/margarine					**Fat**			
							Total	

Sweets & Snacks (Sparingly)					**Servings Per Week/Day:**			
1 piece of candy, 1 serving of fast food, 1 serving of snack foods					**Fat**			
							Total	

Beverages/Water (8-10 cups)					**Servings Per Week/Day:**			
1 cup of water (Track your soda, coffee, tea, & alcohol calories here)								
							Total	

Difference: _____   Total Calories: _____

Supplements

Mood and Complexion

Mood		Complexion	
Notes:			

Exercise Page - Week Two - Day 3

Date: _____   Calories Burned: _____

Remember to warm up prior to exercising!

Cardio Training			Strength Training	
Time	Distance	Cal Burn	Time	Increases

Muscle Group	Weight	Repetitions
Upper Body Exercises		
Neck		
Delts (upper arm)		
Traps (Upper back)		
Pecs (chest)		
Biceps (front arm)		
Triceps (back arm)		
Oblique (waist)		
Abs (stomach)		
Lats (middle back)		
Lower Body Exercises		
Lower Back		
Inner Thigh		
Outer Thigh		
Quads (front thigh)		
Gluts (buttocks)		
Hamstring (back thigh)		
Calves (lower back leg)		
Push-ups		
Sit-ups		
Lunges		
Squats		

Diet Page - Week Two - Day 4

Calorie Intake Required: _____   Date: _____

Fruits (2-4 Servings)						Servings Per Week/Day:	
1 piece, 1/2 cup canned, 1 oz dried, 6 oz juice					Fat Calories		
						Total	

Vegetables (3-5 Servings)						Servings Per Week/Day:	
1 piece, 1 cup raw, 1/2 cup canned, 1 oz dried, 6 oz juice						Fat	
						Total	

Whole Grains (6-11 servings)						Servings Per Week/Day:	
1 slice bread, 1/2 muffin/bun/bagel/tortilla, 1/2 c. pasta/rice, 1oz b/fast cereal						Fat	
						Total	

Meats, Beans, Eggs (2-3 Servings)						Servings Per Week/Day:	
1 egg, 3 oz of meat/fish/poultry, 15 nuts, 1 cup beans						Fat	
						Total	

Dairy Products (2-3 servings)						Servings Per Week/Day:	
1 cup milk, 1 oz cheese, 1 cup yogurt						Fat	
						Total	

Fats, Oil, Butters (Sparingly)						Servings Per Week/Day:	
1 Tbsp for oils, dressings, mayo, nut butters and butter/margarine						Fat	
						Total	

Sweets & Snacks (Sparingly)						Servings Per Week/Day:	
1 piece of candy, 1 serving of fast food, 1 serving of snack foods						Fat	
						Total	

Beverages/Water (8-10 cups)						Servings Per Week/Day:	
1 cup of water (Track your soda, coffee, tea, & alcohol calories here)							
						Total	

Difference: _____   Total Calories: _____

Supplements

Mood and Complexion

Mood		Complexion	
Notes:			

Exercise Page - Week Two - Day 4

Date: _____   Calories Burned: _____

Remember to warm up prior to exercising!

Cardio Training			Strength Training	
Time	Distance	Cal Burn	Time	Increases

Muscle Group	Weight	Repetitions
Upper Body Exercises		
Neck		
Delts (upper arm)		
Traps (Upper back)		
Pecs (chest)		
Biceps (front arm)		
Triceps (back arm)		
Oblique (waist)		
Abs (stomach)		
Lats (middle back)		
Lower Body Exercises		
Lower Back		
Inner Thigh		
Outer Thigh		
Quads (front thigh)		
Gluts (buttocks)		
Hamstring (back thigh)		
Calves (lower back leg)		
Push-ups		
Sit-ups		
Lunges		
Squats		

Diet Page - Week Two - Day 5

Calorie Intake Required: _____   Date: _____

Fruits (2-4 Servings)						Servings Per Week/Day:		
1 piece, 1/2 cup canned, 1 oz dried, 6 oz juice						Fat Calories		
							Total	

Vegetables (3-5 Servings)						Servings Per Week/Day:		
1 piece, 1 cup raw, 1/2 cup canned, 1 oz dried, 6 oz juice							Fat	
							Total	

Whole Grains (6-11 servings)						Servings Per Week/Day:		
1 slice bread, 1/2 muffin/bun/bagel/tortilla, 1/2 c. pasta/rice, 1oz b/fast cereal							Fat	
							Total	

Meats, Beans, Eggs (2-3 Servings)						Servings Per Week/Day:		
1 egg, 3 oz of meat/fish/poultry, 15 nuts, 1 cup beans							Fat	
							Total	

Dairy Products (2-3 servings)						Servings Per Week/Day:		
1 cup milk, 1 oz cheese, 1 cup yogurt							Fat	
							Total	

Fats, Oil, Butters (Sparingly)						Servings Per Week/Day:		
1 Tbsp for oils, dressings, mayo, nut butters and butter/margarine							Fat	
							Total	

Sweets & Snacks (Sparingly)						Servings Per Week/Day:		
1 piece of candy, 1 serving of fast food, 1 serving of snack foods							Fat	
							Total	

Beverages/Water (8-10 cups)						Servings Per Week/Day:		
1 cup of water (Track your soda, coffee, tea, & alcohol calories here)								
							Total	

Difference: _____   Total Calories: _____

Supplements

Mood and Complexion

Mood		Complexion	
Notes:			

Exercise Page - Week Two - Day 5

Date: _____   Calories Burned: _____

Remember to warm up prior to exercising!

Cardio Training			Strength Training	
Time	Distance	Cal Burn	Time	Increases

Muscle Group	Weight	Repetitions
Upper Body Exercises		
Neck		
Delts (upper arm)		
Traps (Upper back)		
Pecs (chest)		
Biceps (front arm)		
Triceps (back arm)		
Oblique (waist)		
Abs (stomach)		
Lats (middle back)		
Lower Body Exercises		
Lower Back		
Inner Thigh		
Outer Thigh		
Quads (front thigh)		
Gluts (buttocks)		
Hamstring (back thigh)		
Calves (lower back leg)		
Push-ups		
Sit-ups		
Lunges		
Squats		

Diet Page - Week Two - Day 6

Calorie Intake Required: _____   Date: _____

Fruits (2-4 Servings)						Servings Per Week/Day:		
1 piece, 1/2 cup canned, 1 oz dried, 6 oz juice						Fat Calories		
							Total	

Vegetables (3-5 Servings)						Servings Per Week/Day:		
1 piece, 1 cup raw, 1/2 cup canned, 1 oz dried, 6 oz juice							Fat	
							Total	

Whole Grains (6-11 servings)						Servings Per Week/Day:		
1 slice bread, 1/2 muffin/bun/bagel/tortilla, 1/2 c. pasta/rice, 1oz b/fast cereal							Fat	
							Total	

Meats, Beans, Eggs (2-3 Servings)						Servings Per Week/Day:		
1 egg, 3 oz of meat/fish/poultry, 15 nuts, 1 cup beans							Fat	
							Total	

Dairy Products (2-3 servings)						Servings Per Week/Day:		
1 cup milk, 1 oz cheese, 1 cup yogurt							Fat	
							Total	

Fats, Oil, Butters (Sparingly)						Servings Per Week/Day:		
1 Tbsp for oils, dressings, mayo, nut butters and butter/margarine							Fat	
							Total	

Sweets & Snacks (Sparingly)						Servings Per Week/Day:		
1 piece of candy, 1 serving of fast food, 1 serving of snack foods							Fat	
							Total	

Beverages/Water (8-10 cups)						Servings Per Week/Day:		
1 cup of water (Track your soda, coffee, tea, & alcohol calories here)								
							Total	

Difference: _____   Total Calories: _____

Supplements

Mood and Complexion

Mood		Complexion	
Notes:			

Exercise Page - Week Two - Day 6

Date: _____   Calories Burned: _____

Remember to warm up prior to exercising!

Cardio Training			Strength Training	
Time	Distance	Cal Burn	Time	Increases

Muscle Group	Weight	Repetitions
Upper Body Exercises		
Neck		
Delts (upper arm)		
Traps (Upper back)		
Pecs (chest)		
Biceps (front arm)		
Triceps (back arm)		
Oblique (waist)		
Abs (stomach)		
Lats (middle back)		
Lower Body Exercises		
Lower Back		
Inner Thigh		
Outer Thigh		
Quads (front thigh)		
Gluts (buttocks)		
Hamstring (back thigh)		
Calves (lower back leg)		
Push-ups		
Sit-ups		
Lunges		
Squats		

Diet Page - Week Two - Day 7

Calorie Intake Required: _____   Date: _____

Fruits (2-4 Servings)						Servings Per Week/Day:		
1 piece, 1/2 cup canned, 1 oz dried, 6 oz juice						**Fat Calories**		
							Total	

Vegetables (3-5 Servings)						Servings Per Week/Day:		
1 piece, 1 cup raw, 1/2 cup canned, 1 oz dried, 6 oz juice							**Fat**	
							Total	

Whole Grains (6-11 servings)						Servings Per Week/Day:		
1 slice bread, 1/2 muffin/bun/bagel/tortilla, 1/2 c. pasta/rice, 1oz b/fast cereal							**Fat**	
							Total	

Meats, Beans, Eggs (2-3 Servings)						Servings Per Week/Day:		
1 egg, 3 oz of meat/fish/poultry, 15 nuts, 1 cup beans							**Fat**	
							Total	

Dairy Products (2-3 servings)						Servings Per Week/Day:		
1 cup milk, 1 oz cheese, 1 cup yogurt							**Fat**	
							Total	

Fats, Oil, Butters (Sparingly)						Servings Per Week/Day:		
1 Tbsp for oils, dressings, mayo, nut butters and butter/margarine							**Fat**	
							Total	

Sweets & Snacks (Sparingly)						Servings Per Week/Day:		
1 piece of candy, 1 serving of fast food, 1 serving of snack foods							**Fat**	
							Total	

Beverages/Water (8-10 cups)						Servings Per Week/Day:		
1 cup of water (Track your soda, coffee, tea, & alcohol calories here)								
							Total	

Difference: _____   Total Calories: _____

Supplements

Mood and Complexion

Mood		Complexion	
Notes:			

Exercise Page - Week Two - Day 7

Date: _____   Calories Burned: _____

Remember to warm up prior to exercising!

Cardio Training			Strength Training	
Time	Distance	Cal Burn	Time	Increases

Muscle Group	Weight	Repetitions
Upper Body Exercises		
Neck		
Delts (upper arm)		
Traps (Upper back)		
Pecs (chest)		
Biceps (front arm)		
Triceps (back arm)		
Oblique (waist)		
Abs (stomach)		
Lats (middle back)		
Lower Body Exercises		
Lower Back		
Inner Thigh		
Outer Thigh		
Quads (front thigh)		
Gluts (buttocks)		
Hamstring (back thigh)		
Calves (lower back leg)		
Push-ups		
Sit-ups		
Lunges		
Squats		

Formula Page   Date: _____

Use this page to recalculate when you've lost weight!

_____ × _____ = _____
Current Weight   Activity Multiplier   Calories Required for this weight

_____ × _____ = _____
Healthy Weight   Activity Multiplier   Calories Required for this weight

_____
Difference

3500/_____ = _____
   Difference   Days to lose 1 pound of body fat

To recalculate with exercising:

_____ × 7 = _____ calories reduced per week
Difference

_____ × _____ = _____ extra calories burned per week
Activity   Days per week

_____ + _____ = _____ / 7 = _____
Reduced Calories   Extra Calories Burned   Total for the Week   avg reduced per day

3500/_____ = _____
   Avg reduced per day   Days to lose 1 pound of body fat

Notes:

Day Of Week	Intake Calories	Burned Calories
Sunday		
Monday		
Tuesday		
Wednesday		
Thursday		
Friday		
Saturday		
Totals		

Tracking Pages
Week Three

Did you …

- Write your measurements on the Progress Chart?

- Figure out your eating habits?

- Make adjustments to your routine by just looking at your diet?

- Go grocery shopping?

- Decide to make any changes in your tracking method?

Remember …

- Your body is <u>still</u> in its "former" phase. It takes around four weeks for me to notice some changes. It may take you more or less! Don't be disappointed if your measurements aren't changing according to your plans. At the start of week three, I was up another 4 pounds, and ready to bust out of my "fat" pants. Hang tough. Remember, I didn't know about the salt thing yet!

Write down the changes you noticed after week two here. If you try another diet plan, you will have these notes to compare your progress at this point in the diet.

Diet Page - Week Three - Day 1

Calorie Intake Required: _____   Date: _____

Fruits (2-4 Servings)				Servings Per Week/Day:			
1 piece, 1/2 cup canned, 1 oz dried, 6 oz juice				Fat Calories			
						Total	

Vegetables (3-5 Servings)				Servings Per Week/Day:			
1 piece, 1 cup raw, 1/2 cup canned, 1 oz dried, 6 oz juice				Fat			
						Total	

Whole Grains (6-11 servings)				Servings Per Week/Day:			
1 slice bread, 1/2 muffin/bun/bagel/tortilla, 1/2 c. pasta/rice, 1oz b/fast cereal				Fat			
						Total	

Meats, Beans, Eggs (2-3 Servings)				Servings Per Week/Day:			
1 egg, 3 oz of meat/fish/poultry, 15 nuts, 1 cup beans				Fat			
						Total	

Dairy Products (2-3 servings)				Servings Per Week/Day:			
1 cup milk, 1 oz cheese, 1 cup yogurt				Fat			
						Total	

Fats, Oil, Butters (Sparingly)				Servings Per Week/Day:			
1 Tbsp for oils, dressings, mayo, nut butters and butter/margarine				Fat			
						Total	

Sweets & Snacks (Sparingly)				Servings Per Week/Day:			
1 piece of candy, 1 serving of fast food, 1 serving of snack foods				Fat			
						Total	

Beverages/Water (8-10 cups)				Servings Per Week/Day:			
1 cup of water (Track your soda, coffee, tea, & alcohol calories here)							
						Total	

Difference: _____   Total Calories: _____

Supplements

Mood and Complexion

Mood		Complexion	
Notes:			

Exercise Page - Week Three - Day 1

Date: _____   Calories Burned: _____

Remember to warm up prior to exercising!

Cardio Training			Strength Training	
Time	Distance	Cal Burn	Time	Increases

Muscle Group	Weight	Repetitions
Upper Body Exercises		
Neck		
Delts (upper arm)		
Traps (Upper back)		
Pecs (chest)		
Biceps (front arm)		
Triceps (back arm)		
Oblique (waist)		
Abs (stomach)		
Lats (middle back)		
Lower Body Exercises		
Lower Back		
Inner Thigh		
Outer Thigh		
Quads (front thigh)		
Gluts (buttocks)		
Hamstring (back thigh)		
Calves (lower back leg)		
Push-ups		
Sit-ups		
Lunges		
Squats		

Diet Page - Week Three - Day 2

Calorie Intake Required: _____   Date: _____

Fruits (2-4 Servings)						Servings Per Week/Day:		
1 piece, 1/2 cup canned, 1 oz dried, 6 oz juice						**Fat Calories**		
							Total	

Vegetables (3-5 Servings)						Servings Per Week/Day:		
1 piece, 1 cup raw, 1/2 cup canned, 1 oz dried, 6 oz juice							**Fat**	
							Total	

Whole Grains (6-11 servings)						Servings Per Week/Day:		
1 slice bread, 1/2 muffin/bun/bagel/tortilla, 1/2 c. pasta/rice, 1oz b/fast cereal							**Fat**	
							Total	

Meats,Beans, Eggs (2-3 Servings)						Servings Per Week/Day:		
1 egg, 3 oz of meat/fish/poultry, 15 nuts, 1 cup beans							**Fat**	
							Total	

Dairy Products (2-3 servings)						Servings Per Week/Day:		
1 cup milk, 1 oz cheese, 1 cup yogurt							**Fat**	
							Total	

Fats, Oil, Butters (Sparingly)						Servings Per Week/Day:		
1 Tbsp for oils, dressings, mayo, nut butters and butter/margarine							**Fat**	
							Total	

Sweets & Snacks (Sparingly)						Servings Per Week/Day:		
1 piece of candy, 1 serving of fast food, 1 serving of snack foods							**Fat**	
							Total	

Beverages/Water (8-10 cups)						Servings Per Week/Day:		
1 cup of water (Track your soda, coffee, tea, & alcohol calories here)								
							Total	

Difference: _____   Total Calories: _____

Supplements

Mood and Complexion

Mood		Complexion	
Notes:			

Exercise Page - Week Three - Day 2

Date: _____   Calories Burned: _____

Remember to warm up prior to exercising!

Cardio Training			Strength Training	
Time	Distance	Cal Burn	Time	Increases

Muscle Group	Weight	Repetitions
Upper Body Exercises		
Neck		
Delts (upper arm)		
Traps (Upper back)		
Pecs (chest)		
Biceps (front arm)		
Triceps (back arm)		
Oblique (waist)		
Abs (stomach)		
Lats (middle back)		
Lower Body Exercises		
Lower Back		
Inner Thigh		
Outer Thigh		
Quads (front thigh)		
Gluts (buttocks)		
Hamstring (back thigh)		
Calves (lower back leg)		
Push-ups		
Sit-ups		
Lunges		
Squats		

Diet Page - Week Three - Day 3

Calorie Intake Required: _____   Date: _____

Fruits (2-4 Servings)						Servings Per Week/Day:		
1 piece, 1/2 cup canned, 1 oz dried, 6 oz juice						Fat Calories		
							Total	

Vegetables (3-5 Servings)						Servings Per Week/Day:		
1 piece, 1 cup raw, 1/2 cup canned, 1 oz dried, 6 oz juice							Fat	
							Total	

Whole Grains (6-11 servings)						Servings Per Week/Day:		
1 slice bread, 1/2 muffin/bun/bagel/tortilla, 1/2 c. pasta/rice, 1oz b/fast cereal							Fat	
							Total	

Meats, Beans, Eggs (2-3 Servings)						Servings Per Week/Day:		
1 egg, 3 oz of meat/fish/poultry, 15 nuts, 1 cup beans							Fat	
							Total	

Dairy Products (2-3 servings)						Servings Per Week/Day:		
1 cup milk, 1 oz cheese, 1 cup yogurt							Fat	
							Total	

Fats, Oil, Butters (Sparingly)						Servings Per Week/Day:		
1 Tbsp for oils, dressings, mayo, nut butters and butter/margarine							Fat	
							Total	

Sweets & Snacks (Sparingly)						Servings Per Week/Day:		
1 piece of candy, 1 serving of fast food, 1 serving of snack foods							Fat	
							Total	

Beverages/Water (8-10 cups)						Servings Per Week/Day:		
1 cup of water (Track your soda, coffee, tea, & alcohol calories here)								
							Total	

Difference: _____   Total Calories: _____

Supplements

Mood and Complexion

Mood		Complexion	
Notes:			

Exercise Page - Week Three - Day 3

Date: _____   Calories Burned: _____

Remember to warm up prior to exercising!

Cardio Training			Strength Training	
Time	Distance	Cal Burn	Time	Increases

Muscle Group	Weight	Repetitions
Upper Body Exercises		
Neck		
Delts (upper arm)		
Traps (Upper back)		
Pecs (chest)		
Biceps (front arm)		
Triceps (back arm)		
Oblique (waist)		
Abs (stomach)		
Lats (middle back)		
Lower Body Exercises		
Lower Back		
Inner Thigh		
Outer Thigh		
Quads (front thigh)		
Gluts (buttocks)		
Hamstring (back thigh)		
Calves (lower back leg)		
Push-ups		
Sit-ups		
Lunges		
Squats		

Diet Page - Week Three - Day 4

Calorie Intake Required: _____   Date: _____

Fruits (2-4 Servings)					Servings Per Week/Day:			
1 piece, 1/2 cup canned, 1 oz dried, 6 oz juice					**Fat Calories**			
							Total	

Vegetables (3-5 Servings)					Servings Per Week/Day:			
1 piece, 1 cup raw, 1/2 cup canned, 1 oz dried, 6 oz juice							**Fat**	
							Total	

Whole Grains (6-11 servings)					Servings Per Week/Day:			
1 slice bread, 1/2 muffin/bun/bagel/tortilla, 1/2 c. pasta/rice, 1oz b/fast cereal							**Fat**	
							Total	

Meats, Beans, Eggs (2-3 Servings)					Servings Per Week/Day:			
1 egg, 3 oz of meat/fish/poultry, 15 nuts, 1 cup beans							**Fat**	
							Total	

Dairy Products (2-3 servings)					Servings Per Week/Day:			
1 cup milk, 1 oz cheese, 1 cup yogurt							**Fat**	
							Total	

Fats, Oil, Butters (Sparingly)					Servings Per Week/Day:			
1 Tbsp for oils, dressings, mayo, nut butters and butter/margarine							**Fat**	
							Total	

Sweets & Snacks (Sparingly)					Servings Per Week/Day:			
1 piece of candy, 1 serving of fast food, 1 serving of snack foods							**Fat**	
							Total	

Beverages/Water (8-10 cups)					Servings Per Week/Day:			
1 cup of water (Track your soda, coffee, tea, & alcohol calories here)								
							Total	

Difference: _____   Total Calories: _____

Supplements

Mood and Complexion

Mood		Complexion	
Notes:			

Exercise Page - Week Three - Day 4

Date: _____   Calories Burned: _____

Remember to warm up prior to exercising!

Cardio Training			Strength Training	
Time	Distance	Cal Burn	Time	Increases

Muscle Group	Weight	Repetitions
Upper Body Exercises		
Neck		
Delts (upper arm)		
Traps (Upper back)		
Pecs (chest)		
Biceps (front arm)		
Triceps (back arm)		
Oblique (waist)		
Abs (stomach)		
Lats (middle back)		
Lower Body Exercises		
Lower Back		
Inner Thigh		
Outer Thigh		
Quads (front thigh)		
Gluts (buttocks)		
Hamstring (back thigh)		
Calves (lower back leg)		
Push-ups		
Sit-ups		
Lunges		
Squats		

Diet Page - Week Three - Day 5

Calorie Intake Required: _____   Date: _____

Fruits (2-4 Servings)						Servings Per Week/Day:		
1 piece, 1/2 cup canned, 1 oz dried, 6 oz juice						**Fat Calories**		
							Total	

Vegetables (3-5 Servings)						Servings Per Week/Day:		
1 piece, 1 cup raw, 1/2 cup canned, 1 oz dried, 6 oz juice							Fat	
							Total	

Whole Grains (6-11 servings)						Servings Per Week/Day:		
1 slice bread, 1/2 muffin/bun/bagel/tortilla, 1/2 c. pasta/rice, 1oz b/fast cereal							Fat	
							Total	

Meats,Beans, Eggs (2-3 Servings)						Servings Per Week/Day:		
1 egg, 3 oz of meat/fish/poultry, 15 nuts, 1 cup beans							Fat	
							Total	

Dairy Products (2-3 servings)						Servings Per Week/Day:		
1 cup milk, 1 oz cheese, 1 cup yogurt							Fat	
							Total	

Fats, Oil, Butters (Sparingly)						Servings Per Week/Day:		
1 Tbsp for oils, dressings, mayo, nut butters and butter/margarine							Fat	
							Total	

Sweets & Snacks (Sparingly)						Servings Per Week/Day:		
1 piece of candy, 1 serving of fast food, 1 serving of snack foods							Fat	
							Total	

Beverages/Water (8-10 cups)						Servings Per Week/Day:		
1 cup of water (Track your soda, coffee, tea, & alcohol calories here)								
							Total	

Difference: _____   Total Calories: _____

Supplements

Mood and Complexion

Mood		Complexion	
Notes:			

Exercise Page - Week Three - Day 5

Date: _____   Calories Burned: _____

Remember to warm up prior to exercising!

Cardio Training			Strength Training	
Time	Distance	Cal Burn	Time	Increases

Muscle Group	Weight	Repetitions
Upper Body Exercises		
Neck		
Delts (upper arm)		
Traps (Upper back)		
Pecs (chest)		
Biceps (front arm)		
Triceps (back arm)		
Oblique (waist)		
Abs (stomach)		
Lats (middle back)		
Lower Body Exercises		
Lower Back		
Inner Thigh		
Outer Thigh		
Quads (front thigh)		
Gluts (buttocks)		
Hamstring (back thigh)		
Calves (lower back leg)		
Push-ups		
Sit-ups		
Lunges		
Squats		

Diet Page - Week Three - Day 6

Calorie Intake Required: _____   Date: _____

Fruits (2-4 Servings)					Servings Per Week/Day:			
1 piece, 1/2 cup canned, 1 oz dried, 6 oz juice					**Fat Calories**			
							Total	

Vegetables (3-5 Servings)					Servings Per Week/Day:			
1 piece, 1 cup raw, 1/2 cup canned, 1 oz dried, 6 oz juice							**Fat**	
							Total	

Whole Grains (6-11 servings)					Servings Per Week/Day:			
1 slice bread, 1/2 muffin/bun/bagel/tortilla, 1/2 c. pasta/rice, 1oz b/fast cereal							**Fat**	
							Total	

Meats, Beans, Eggs (2-3 Servings)					Servings Per Week/Day:			
1 egg, 3 oz of meat/fish/poultry, 15 nuts, 1 cup beans							**Fat**	
							Total	

Dairy Products (2-3 servings)					Servings Per Week/Day:			
1 cup milk, 1 oz cheese, 1 cup yogurt							**Fat**	
							Total	

Fats, Oil, Butters (Sparingly)					Servings Per Week/Day:			
1 Tbsp for oils, dressings, mayo, nut butters and butter/margarine							**Fat**	
							Total	

Sweets & Snacks (Sparingly)					Servings Per Week/Day:			
1 piece of candy, 1 serving of fast food, 1 serving of snack foods							**Fat**	
							Total	

Beverages/Water (8-10 cups)					Servings Per Week/Day:			
1 cup of water (Track your soda, coffee, tea, & alcohol calories here)								
							Total	

Difference: _____   Total Calories: _____

Supplements

Mood and Complexion

Mood		Complexion	
Notes:			

Exercise Page - Week Three - Day 6

Date: _____   Calories Burned: _____

Remember to warm up prior to exercising!

Cardio Training			Strength Training	
Time	Distance	Cal Burn	Time	Increases

Muscle Group	Weight	Repetitions
Upper Body Exercises		
Neck		
Delts (upper arm)		
Traps (Upper back)		
Pecs (chest)		
Biceps (front arm)		
Triceps (back arm)		
Oblique (waist)		
Abs (stomach)		
Lats (middle back)		
Lower Body Exercises		
Lower Back		
Inner Thigh		
Outer Thigh		
Quads (front thigh)		
Gluts (buttocks)		
Hamstring (back thigh)		
Calves (lower back leg)		
Push-ups		
Sit-ups		
Lunges		
Squats		

Diet Page - Week Three - Day 7

Calorie Intake Required: _____   Date: _____

Fruits (2-4 Servings)						Servings Per Week/Day:		
1 piece, 1/2 cup canned, 1 oz dried, 6 oz juice						**Fat Calories**		
							Total	

Vegetables (3-5 Servings)						Servings Per Week/Day:		
1 piece, 1 cup raw, 1/2 cup canned, 1 oz dried, 6 oz juice							**Fat**	
							Total	

Whole Grains (6-11 servings)						Servings Per Week/Day:		
1 slice bread, 1/2 muffin/bun/bagel/tortilla, 1/2 c. pasta/rice, 1oz b/fast cereal							**Fat**	
							Total	

Meats,Beans, Eggs (2-3 Servings)						Servings Per Week/Day:		
1 egg, 3 oz of meat/fish/poultry, 15 nuts, 1 cup beans							**Fat**	
							Total	

Dairy Products (2-3 servings)						Servings Per Week/Day:		
1 cup milk, 1 oz cheese, 1 cup yogurt							**Fat**	
							Total	

Fats, Oil, Butters (Sparingly)						Servings Per Week/Day:		
1 Tbsp for oils, dressings, mayo, nut butters and butter/margarine							**Fat**	
							Total	

Sweets & Snacks (Sparingly)						Servings Per Week/Day:		
1 piece of candy, 1 serving of fast food, 1 serving of snack foods							**Fat**	
							Total	

Beverages/Water (8-10 cups)						Servings Per Week/Day:		
1 cup of water (Track your soda, coffee, tea, & alcohol calories here)								
							Total	

Difference: _____   Total Calories: _____

Supplements

Mood and Complexion

Mood		Complexion	
Notes:			

Exercise Page - Week Three - Day 7

Date: _____   Calories Burned: _____

Remember to warm up prior to exercising!

Cardio Training			Strength Training	
Time	Distance	Cal Burn	Time	Increases

Muscle Group	Weight	Repetitions
Upper Body Exercises		
Neck		
Delts (upper arm)		
Traps (Upper back)		
Pecs (chest)		
Biceps (front arm)		
Triceps (back arm)		
Oblique (waist)		
Abs (stomach)		
Lats (middle back)		
Lower Body Exercises		
Lower Back		
Inner Thigh		
Outer Thigh		
Quads (front thigh)		
Gluts (buttocks)		
Hamstring (back thigh)		
Calves (lower back leg)		
Push-ups		
Sit-ups		
Lunges		
Squats		

Notes:

Day Of Week	Intake Calories	Burned Calories
Sunday		
Monday		
Tuesday		
Wednesday		
Thursday		
Friday		
Saturday		
Totals		

Tracking Pages
Week Four

Did you …
- Write your measurements on the Progress Chart?
- Go grocery shopping?
- Make adjustments to your routines?
- Recalculate your formulas from the diet tips section if you're counting calories?

Remember …
- Your body should be starting to realize something is up. Your skin should be hydrated. You may notice breakouts as your body starts flushing out toxins. I felt like I was going through puberty again during the first month of healthy eating. It will clear up!
- You should be seeing an increase in your cardio time and increases in the amount of weight in your workout.

Write down the changes you noticed after week three.

Diet Page - Week Four - Day 1

Calorie Intake Required: _____   Date: _____

Fruits (2-4 Servings)					Servings Per Week/Day:		
1 piece, 1/2 cup canned, 1 oz dried, 6 oz juice					Fat Calories		
						Total	

Vegetables (3-5 Servings)					Servings Per Week/Day:		
1 piece, 1 cup raw, 1/2 cup canned, 1 oz dried, 6 oz juice						Fat	
						Total	

Whole Grains (6-11 servings)					Servings Per Week/Day:		
1 slice bread, 1/2 muffin/bun/bagel/tortilla, 1/2 c. pasta/rice, 1oz b/fast cereal						Fat	
						Total	

Meats, Beans, Eggs (2-3 Servings)					Servings Per Week/Day:		
1 egg, 3 oz of meat/fish/poultry, 15 nuts, 1 cup beans						Fat	
						Total	

Dairy Products (2-3 servings)					Servings Per Week/Day:		
1 cup milk, 1 oz cheese, 1 cup yogurt						Fat	
						Total	

Fats, Oil, Butters (Sparingly)					Servings Per Week/Day:		
1 Tbsp for oils, dressings, mayo, nut butters and butter/margarine						Fat	
						Total	

Sweets & Snacks (Sparingly)					Servings Per Week/Day:		
1 piece of candy, 1 serving of fast food, 1 serving of snack foods						Fat	
						Total	

Beverages/Water (8-10 cups)					Servings Per Week/Day:		
1 cup of water (Track your soda, coffee, tea, & alcohol calories here)							
						Total	

Difference: _____   Total Calories: _____

Supplements

Mood and Complexion

Mood		Complexion	
Notes:			

Exercise Page - Week Four - Day 1

Date: _____   Calories Burned: _____

Remember to warm up prior to exercising!

Cardio Training			Strength Training	
Time	Distance	Cal Burn	Time	Increases

Muscle Group	Weight	Repetitions
Upper Body Exercises		
Neck		
Delts (upper arm)		
Traps (Upper back)		
Pecs (chest)		
Biceps (front arm)		
Triceps (back arm)		
Oblique (waist)		
Abs (stomach)		
Lats (middle back)		
Lower Body Exercises		
Lower Back		
Inner Thigh		
Outer Thigh		
Quads (front thigh)		
Gluts (buttocks)		
Hamstring (back thigh)		
Calves (lower back leg)		
Push-ups		
Sit-ups		
Lunges		
Squats		

Diet Page - Week Four - Day 2

Calorie Intake Required: _____   Date: _____

Fruits (2-4 Servings)					Servings Per Week/Day:				
1 piece, 1/2 cup canned, 1 oz dried, 6 oz juice					**Fat Calories**				
								Total	

Vegetables (3-5 Servings)					Servings Per Week/Day:				
1 piece, 1 cup raw, 1/2 cup canned, 1 oz dried, 6 oz juice							**Fat**		
								Total	

Whole Grains (6-11 servings)					Servings Per Week/Day:				
1 slice bread, 1/2 muffin/bun/bagel/tortilla, 1/2 c. pasta/rice, 1oz b/fast cereal							**Fat**		
								Total	

Meats, Beans, Eggs (2-3 Servings)					Servings Per Week/Day:				
1 egg, 3 oz of meat/fish/poultry, 15 nuts, 1 cup beans							**Fat**		
								Total	

Dairy Products (2-3 servings)					Servings Per Week/Day:				
1 cup milk, 1 oz cheese, 1 cup yogurt							**Fat**		
								Total	

Fats, Oil, Butters (Sparingly)					Servings Per Week/Day:				
1 Tbsp for oils, dressings, mayo, nut butters and butter/margarine							**Fat**		
								Total	

Sweets & Snacks (Sparingly)					Servings Per Week/Day:				
1 piece of candy, 1 serving of fast food, 1 serving of snack foods							**Fat**		
								Total	

Beverages/Water (8-10 cups)					Servings Per Week/Day:				
1 cup of water (Track your soda, coffee, tea, & alcohol calories here)									
								Total	

Difference: _____   Total Calories: _____

Supplements

Mood and Complexion

Mood		Complexion	
Notes:			

Exercise Page - Week Four - Day 2

Date: _____   Calories Burned: _____

Remember to warm up prior to exercising!

Cardio Training			Strength Training	
Time	Distance	Cal Burn	Time	Increases

Muscle Group	Weight	Repetitions
Upper Body Exercises		
Neck		
Delts (upper arm)		
Traps (Upper back)		
Pecs (chest)		
Biceps (front arm)		
Triceps (back arm)		
Oblique (waist)		
Abs (stomach)		
Lats (middle back)		
Lower Body Exercises		
Lower Back		
Inner Thigh		
Outer Thigh		
Quads (front thigh)		
Gluts (buttocks)		
Hamstring (back thigh)		
Calves (lower back leg)		
Push-ups		
Sit-ups		
Lunges		
Squats		

Diet Page - Week Four - Day 3

Calorie Intake Required: _____   Date: _____

Fruits (2-4 Servings)						Servings Per Week/Day:		
1 piece, 1/2 cup canned, 1 oz dried, 6 oz juice						Fat Calories		
							Total	

Vegetables (3-5 Servings)						Servings Per Week/Day:		
1 piece, 1 cup raw, 1/2 cup canned, 1 oz dried, 6 oz juice							Fat	
							Total	

Whole Grains (6-11 servings)						Servings Per Week/Day:		
1 slice bread, 1/2 muffin/bun/bagel/tortilla, 1/2 c. pasta/rice, 1oz b/fast cereal							Fat	
							Total	

Meats, Beans, Eggs (2-3 Servings)						Servings Per Week/Day:		
1 egg, 3 oz of meat/fish/poultry, 15 nuts, 1 cup beans							Fat	
							Total	

Dairy Products (2-3 servings)						Servings Per Week/Day:		
1 cup milk, 1 oz cheese, 1 cup yogurt							Fat	
							Total	

Fats, Oil, Butters (Sparingly)						Servings Per Week/Day:		
1 Tbsp for oils, dressings, mayo, nut butters and butter/margarine							Fat	
							Total	

Sweets & Snacks (Sparingly)						Servings Per Week/Day:		
1 piece of candy, 1 serving of fast food, 1 serving of snack foods							Fat	
							Total	

Beverages/Water (8-10 cups)						Servings Per Week/Day:		
1 cup of water (Track your soda, coffee, tea, & alcohol calories here)								
							Total	

Difference: _____   Total Calories: _____

Supplements

Mood and Complexion

Mood		Complexion	
Notes:			

Exercise Page - Week Four - Day 3

Date: _____   Calories Burned: _____

Remember to warm up prior to exercising!

Cardio Training			Strength Training	
Time	Distance	Cal Burn	Time	Increases

Muscle Group	Weight	Repetitions
Upper Body Exercises		
Neck		
Delts (upper arm)		
Traps (Upper back)		
Pecs (chest)		
Biceps (front arm)		
Triceps (back arm)		
Oblique (waist)		
Abs (stomach)		
Lats (middle back)		
Lower Body Exercises		
Lower Back		
Inner Thigh		
Outer Thigh		
Quads (front thigh)		
Gluts (buttocks)		
Hamstring (back thigh)		
Calves (lower back leg)		
Push-ups		
Sit-ups		
Lunges		
Squats		

Diet Page - Week Four - Day 4

Calorie Intake Required: _____   Date: _____

Fruits (2-4 Servings)	Servings Per Week/Day:							
1 piece, 1/2 cup canned, 1 oz dried, 6 oz juice	Fat Calories							
							Total	

Vegetables (3-5 Servings)	Servings Per Week/Day:							
1 piece, 1 cup raw, 1/2 cup canned, 1 oz dried, 6 oz juice							Fat	
							Total	

Whole Grains (6-11 servings)	Servings Per Week/Day:							
1 slice bread, 1/2 muffin/bun/bagel/tortilla, 1/2 c. pasta/rice, 1oz b/fast cereal							Fat	
							Total	

Meats, Beans, Eggs (2-3 Servings)	Servings Per Week/Day:							
1 egg, 3 oz of meat/fish/poultry, 15 nuts, 1 cup beans							Fat	
							Total	

Dairy Products (2-3 servings)	Servings Per Week/Day:							
1 cup milk, 1 oz cheese, 1 cup yogurt							Fat	
							Total	

Fats, Oil, Butters (Sparingly)	Servings Per Week/Day:							
1 Tbsp for oils, dressings, mayo, nut butters and butter/margarine							Fat	
							Total	

Sweets & Snacks (Sparingly)	Servings Per Week/Day:							
1 piece of candy, 1 serving of fast food, 1 serving of snack foods							Fat	
							Total	

Beverages/Water (8-10 cups)	Servings Per Week/Day:							
1 cup of water (Track your soda, coffee, tea, & alcohol calories here)								
							Total	

Difference: _____   Total Calories: _____

Supplements

Mood and Complexion

Mood		Complexion	
Notes:			

Exercise Page - Week Four - Day 4

Date: _____   Calories Burned: _____

Remember to warm up prior to exercising!

Cardio Training			Strength Training	
Time	Distance	Cal Burn	Time	Increases

Muscle Group	Weight	Repetitions
Upper Body Exercises		
Neck		
Delts (upper arm)		
Traps (Upper back)		
Pecs (chest)		
Biceps (front arm)		
Triceps (back arm)		
Oblique (waist)		
Abs (stomach)		
Lats (middle back)		
Lower Body Exercises		
Lower Back		
Inner Thigh		
Outer Thigh		
Quads (front thigh)		
Gluts (buttocks)		
Hamstring (back thigh)		
Calves (lower back leg)		
Push-ups		
Sit-ups		
Lunges		
Squats		

Diet Page - Week Four - Day 5

Calorie Intake Required: _____   Date: _____

Fruits (2-4 Servings)					Servings Per Week/Day:			
1 piece, 1/2 cup canned, 1 oz dried, 6 oz juice					Fat Calories			
							Total	

Vegetables (3-5 Servings)					Servings Per Week/Day:			
1 piece, 1 cup raw, 1/2 cup canned, 1 oz dried, 6 oz juice							Fat	
							Total	

Whole Grains (6-11 servings)					Servings Per Week/Day:			
1 slice bread, 1/2 muffin/bun/bagel/tortilla, 1/2 c. pasta/rice, 1oz b/fast cereal							Fat	
							Total	

Meats, Beans, Eggs (2-3 Servings)					Servings Per Week/Day:			
1 egg, 3 oz of meat/fish/poultry, 15 nuts, 1 cup beans							Fat	
							Total	

Dairy Products (2-3 servings)					Servings Per Week/Day:			
1 cup milk, 1 oz cheese, 1 cup yogurt							Fat	
							Total	

Fats, Oil, Butters (Sparingly)					Servings Per Week/Day:			
1 Tbsp for oils, dressings, mayo, nut butters and butter/margarine							Fat	
							Total	

Sweets & Snacks (Sparingly)					Servings Per Week/Day:			
1 piece of candy, 1 serving of fast food, 1 serving of snack foods							Fat	
							Total	

Beverages/Water (8-10 cups)					Servings Per Week/Day:			
1 cup of water (Track your soda, coffee, tea, & alcohol calories here)								
							Total	

Difference: _____   Total Calories: _____

Supplements

Mood and Complexion

Mood		Complexion	
Notes:			

Exercise Page - Week Four - Day 5

Date: _____   Calories Burned: _____

Remember to warm up prior to exercising!

Cardio Training			Strength Training	
Time	Distance	Cal Burn	Time	Increases

Muscle Group	Weight	Repetitions
Upper Body Exercises		
Neck		
Delts (upper arm)		
Traps (Upper back)		
Pecs (chest)		
Biceps (front arm)		
Triceps (back arm)		
Oblique (waist)		
Abs (stomach)		
Lats (middle back)		
Lower Body Exercises		
Lower Back		
Inner Thigh		
Outer Thigh		
Quads (front thigh)		
Gluts (buttocks)		
Hamstring (back thigh)		
Calves (lower back leg)		
Push-ups		
Sit-ups		
Lunges		
Squats		

Diet Page - Week Four - Day 6

Calorie Intake Required: _____   Date: _____

Fruits (2-4 Servings)					Servings Per Week/Day:			
1 piece, 1/2 cup canned, 1 oz dried, 6 oz juice					Fat Calories			
							Total	

Vegetables (3-5 Servings)					Servings Per Week/Day:			
1 piece, 1 cup raw, 1/2 cup canned, 1 oz dried, 6 oz juice							Fat	
							Total	

Whole Grains (6-11 servings)					Servings Per Week/Day:			
1 slice bread, 1/2 muffin/bun/bagel/tortilla, 1/2 c. pasta/rice, 1oz b/fast cereal							Fat	
							Total	

Meats,Beans, Eggs (2-3 Servings)					Servings Per Week/Day:			
1 egg, 3 oz of meat/fish/poultry, 15 nuts, 1 cup beans							Fat	
							Total	

Dairy Products (2-3 servings)					Servings Per Week/Day:			
1 cup milk, 1 oz cheese, 1 cup yogurt							Fat	
							Total	

Fats, Oil, Butters (Sparingly)					Servings Per Week/Day:			
1 Tbsp for oils, dressings, mayo, nut butters and butter/margarine							Fat	
							Total	

Sweets & Snacks (Sparingly)					Servings Per Week/Day:			
1 piece of candy, 1 serving of fast food, 1 serving of snack foods							Fat	
							Total	

Beverages/Water (8-10 cups)					Servings Per Week/Day:			
1 cup of water (Track your soda, coffee, tea, & alcohol calories here)								
							Total	

Difference: _____   Total Calories: _____

Supplements

Mood and Complexion

Mood		Complexion	
Notes:			

Exercise Page - Week Four - Day 6

Date: _____   Calories Burned: _____

Remember to warm up prior to exercising!

Cardio Training			Strength Training	
Time	Distance	Cal Burn	Time	Increases

Muscle Group	Weight	Repetitions
Upper Body Exercises		
Neck		
Delts (upper arm)		
Traps (Upper back)		
Pecs (chest)		
Biceps (front arm)		
Triceps (back arm)		
Oblique (waist)		
Abs (stomach)		
Lats (middle back)		
Lower Body Exercises		
Lower Back		
Inner Thigh		
Outer Thigh		
Quads (front thigh)		
Gluts (buttocks)		
Hamstring (back thigh)		
Calves (lower back leg)		
Push-ups		
Sit-ups		
Lunges		
Squats		

Diet Page - Week Four - Day 7

Calorie Intake Required: _____   Date: _____

Fruits (2-4 Servings)	Servings Per Week/Day:							
1 piece, 1/2 cup canned, 1 oz dried, 6 oz juice	Fat Calories							
							Total	

Vegetables (3-5 Servings)	Servings Per Week/Day:							
1 piece, 1 cup raw, 1/2 cup canned, 1 oz dried, 6 oz juice							Fat	
							Total	

Whole Grains (6-11 servings)	Servings Per Week/Day:							
1 slice bread, 1/2 muffin/bun/bagel/tortilla, 1/2 c. pasta/rice, 1oz b/fast cereal							Fat	
							Total	

Meats, Beans, Eggs (2-3 Servings)	Servings Per Week/Day:							
1 egg, 3 oz of meat/fish/poultry, 15 nuts, 1 cup beans							Fat	
							Total	

Dairy Products (2-3 servings)	Servings Per Week/Day:							
1 cup milk, 1 oz cheese, 1 cup yogurt							Fat	
							Total	

Fats, Oil, Butters (Sparingly)	Servings Per Week/Day:							
1 Tbsp for oils, dressings, mayo, nut butters and butter/margarine							Fat	
							Total	

Sweets & Snacks (Sparingly)	Servings Per Week/Day:							
1 piece of candy, 1 serving of fast food, 1 serving of snack foods							Fat	
							Total	

Beverages/Water (8-10 cups)	Servings Per Week/Day:							
1 cup of water (Track your soda, coffee, tea, & alcohol calories here)								
							Total	

Difference: _____   Total Calories: _____

Supplements

Mood and Complexion

Mood		Complexion	
Notes:			

Exercise Page - Week Four - Day 7

Date: _____   Calories Burned: _____

Remember to warm up prior to exercising!

Cardio Training			Strength Training	
Time	Distance	Cal Burn	Time	Increases

Muscle Group	Weight	Repetitions
Upper Body Exercises		
Neck		
Delts (upper arm)		
Traps (Upper back)		
Pecs (chest)		
Biceps (front arm)		
Triceps (back arm)		
Oblique (waist)		
Abs (stomach)		
Lats (middle back)		
Lower Body Exercises		
Lower Back		
Inner Thigh		
Outer Thigh		
Quads (front thigh)		
Gluts (buttocks)		
Hamstring (back thigh)		
Calves (lower back leg)		
Push-ups		
Sit-ups		
Lunges		
Squats		

Formula Page   Date: _____

Use this page to recalculate when you've lost weight!

_____ X _____ = _____
Current Weight   Activity Multiplier   Calories Required for this weight

_____ X _____ = _____
Healthy Weight   Activity Multiplier   Calories Required for this weight

                                    _____
                                    Difference

3500/_____ = _____
         Difference   Days to lose 1 pound of body fat

To recalculate with exercising:

_____ x 7 = _____ calories reduced per week
Difference

_____ X _____ = _____ extra calories burned per week
Activity   Days per week

_____ + _____ = _____ / 7 = _____
Reduced Calories   Extra Calories Burned   Total for the Week   avg reduced per day

3500/_____ = _____
       Avg reduced per day   Days to lose 1 pound of body fat

Notes:

Day Of Week	Intake Calories	Burned Calories
Sunday		
Monday		
Tuesday		
Wednesday		
Thursday		
Friday		
Saturday		
Totals		

Tracking Pages
Week Five

Did you ...

- Write your measurements on the Progress Chart?

- Break out the camera and take some pictures?

- Go grocery shopping?

- Compare your pictures and note the changes? Make adjustments to your routine?

Suggestions: If you want to burn more calories, up your cardio workouts. If you want to tone, increase your exercises. Remember that building muscle burns calories, even while you sleep.

Remember ...

- Your body should be getting used to having a balanced diet and exercise routine. It should start shifting to its "food flow" phase and release stored calories.

- Your clothes should be starting to fit better, and you should be feeling great!

Write your changes below:

Diet Page - Week Five - Day 1

Calorie Intake Required: _____   Date: _____

Fruits (2-4 Servings)					Servings Per Week/Day:			
1 piece, 1/2 cup canned, 1 oz dried, 6 oz juice					Fat Calories			
							Total	

Vegetables (3-5 Servings)					Servings Per Week/Day:			
1 piece, 1 cup raw, 1/2 cup canned, 1 oz dried, 6 oz juice							Fat	
							Total	

Whole Grains (6-11 servings)					Servings Per Week/Day:			
1 slice bread, 1/2 muffin/bun/bagel/tortilla, 1/2 c. pasta/rice, 1oz b/fast cereal							Fat	
							Total	

Meats, Beans, Eggs (2-3 Servings)					Servings Per Week/Day:			
1 egg, 3 oz of meat/fish/poultry, 15 nuts, 1 cup beans							Fat	
							Total	

Dairy Products (2-3 servings)					Servings Per Week/Day:			
1 cup milk, 1 oz cheese, 1 cup yogurt							Fat	
							Total	

Fats, Oil, Butters (Sparingly)					Servings Per Week/Day:			
1 Tbsp for oils, dressings, mayo, nut butters and butter/margarine							Fat	
							Total	

Sweets & Snacks (Sparingly)					Servings Per Week/Day:			
1 piece of candy, 1 serving of fast food, 1 serving of snack foods							Fat	
							Total	

Beverages/Water (8-10 cups)					Servings Per Week/Day:			
1 cup of water (Track your soda, coffee, tea, & alcohol calories here)								
							Total	

Difference: _____   Total Calories: _____

Supplements

Mood and Complexion

Mood		Complexion	
Notes:			

Exercise Page - Week Five - Day 1

Date: _____   Calories Burned: _____

Remember to warm up prior to exercising!

Cardio Training			Strength Training	
Time	Distance	Cal Burn	Time	Increases

Muscle Group	Weight	Repetitions
Upper Body Exercises		
Neck		
Delts (upper arm)		
Traps (Upper back)		
Pecs (chest)		
Biceps (front arm)		
Triceps (back arm)		
Oblique (waist)		
Abs (stomach)		
Lats (middle back)		
Lower Body Exercises		
Lower Back		
Inner Thigh		
Outer Thigh		
Quads (front thigh)		
Gluts (buttocks)		
Hamstring (back thigh)		
Calves (lower back leg)		
Push-ups		
Sit-ups		
Lunges		
Squats		

Diet Page - Week Five - Day 2

Calorie Intake Required: _____   Date: _____

Fruits (2-4 Servings)							Servings Per Week/Day:	
1 piece, 1/2 cup canned, 1 oz dried, 6 oz juice							**Fat Calories**	
							Total	

Vegetables (3-5 Servings)							Servings Per Week/Day:	
1 piece, 1 cup raw, 1/2 cup canned, 1 oz dried, 6 oz juice							**Fat**	
							Total	

Whole Grains (6-11 servings)							Servings Per Week/Day:	
1 slice bread, 1/2 muffin/bun/bagel/tortilla, 1/2 c. pasta/rice, 1oz b/fast cereal							**Fat**	
							Total	

Meats, Beans, Eggs (2-3 Servings)							Servings Per Week/Day:	
1 egg, 3 oz of meat/fish/poultry, 15 nuts, 1 cup beans							**Fat**	
							Total	

Dairy Products (2-3 servings)							Servings Per Week/Day:	
1 cup milk, 1 oz cheese, 1 cup yogurt							**Fat**	
							Total	

Fats, Oil, Butters (Sparingly)							Servings Per Week/Day:	
1 Tbsp for oils, dressings, mayo, nut butters and butter/margarine							**Fat**	
							Total	

Sweets & Snacks (Sparingly)							Servings Per Week/Day:	
1 piece of candy, 1 serving of fast food, 1 serving of snack foods							**Fat**	
							Total	

Beverages/Water (8-10 cups)							Servings Per Week/Day:	
1 cup of water (Track your soda, coffee, tea, & alcohol calories here)								
							Total	

Difference: _____   Total Calories: _____

Supplements

Mood and Complexion

Mood		Complexion	
Notes:			

Exercise Page - Week Five - Day 2

Date: _____   Calories Burned: _____

Remember to warm up prior to exercising!

Cardio Training			Strength Training	
Time	Distance	Cal Burn	Time	Increases

Muscle Group	Weight	Repetitions
Upper Body Exercises		
Neck		
Delts (upper arm)		
Traps (Upper back)		
Pecs (chest)		
Biceps (front arm)		
Triceps (back arm)		
Oblique (waist)		
Abs (stomach)		
Lats (middle back)		
Lower Body Exercises		
Lower Back		
Inner Thigh		
Outer Thigh		
Quads (front thigh)		
Gluts (buttocks)		
Hamstring (back thigh)		
Calves (lower back leg)		
Push-ups		
Sit-ups		
Lunges		
Squats		

Diet Page - Week Five - Day 3

Calorie Intake Required: _____　　Date: _____

Fruits (2-4 Servings)				Servings Per Week/Day:				
1 piece, 1/2 cup canned, 1 oz dried, 6 oz juice				Fat Calories				
							Total	

Vegetables (3-5 Servings)				Servings Per Week/Day:				
1 piece, 1 cup raw, 1/2 cup canned, 1 oz dried, 6 oz juice							Fat	
							Total	

Whole Grains (6-11 servings)				Servings Per Week/Day:				
1 slice bread, 1/2 muffin/bun/bagel/tortilla, 1/2 c. pasta/rice, 1oz b/fast cereal							Fat	
							Total	

Meats, Beans, Eggs (2-3 Servings)				Servings Per Week/Day:				
1 egg, 3 oz of meat/fish/poultry, 15 nuts, 1 cup beans							Fat	
							Total	

Dairy Products (2-3 servings)				Servings Per Week/Day:				
1 cup milk, 1 oz cheese, 1 cup yogurt							Fat	
							Total	

Fats, Oil, Butters (Sparingly)				Servings Per Week/Day:				
1 Tbsp for oils, dressings, mayo, nut butters and butter/margarine							Fat	
							Total	

Sweets & Snacks (Sparingly)				Servings Per Week/Day:				
1 piece of candy, 1 serving of fast food, 1 serving of snack foods							Fat	
							Total	

Beverages/Water (8-10 cups)				Servings Per Week/Day:				
1 cup of water (Track your soda, coffee, tea, & alcohol calories here)								
							Total	

Difference: _____　　　　Total Calories: _____

Supplements

Mood and Complexion

Mood		Complexion	
Notes:			

Exercise Page - Week Five - Day 3

Date: _____   Calories Burned: _____

Remember to warm up prior to exercising!

Cardio Training			Strength Training	
Time	Distance	Cal Burn	Time	Increases

Muscle Group	Weight	Repetitions
Upper Body Exercises		
Neck		
Delts (upper arm)		
Traps (Upper back)		
Pecs (chest)		
Biceps (front arm)		
Triceps (back arm)		
Oblique (waist)		
Abs (stomach)		
Lats (middle back)		
Lower Body Exercises		
Lower Back		
Inner Thigh		
Outer Thigh		
Quads (front thigh)		
Gluts (buttocks)		
Hamstring (back thigh)		
Calves (lower back leg)		
Push-ups		
Sit-ups		
Lunges		
Squats		

Diet Page - Week Five - Day 4

Calorie Intake Required: _____   Date: _____

Fruits (2-4 Servings)						Servings Per Week/Day:		
1 piece, 1/2 cup canned, 1 oz dried, 6 oz juice						Fat Calories		
							Total	

Vegetables (3-5 Servings)						Servings Per Week/Day:		
1 piece, 1 cup raw, 1/2 cup canned, 1 oz dried, 6 oz juice							Fat	
							Total	

Whole Grains (6-11 servings)						Servings Per Week/Day:		
1 slice bread, 1/2 muffin/bun/bagel/tortilla, 1/2 c. pasta/rice, 1oz b/fast cereal							Fat	
							Total	

Meats, Beans, Eggs (2-3 Servings)						Servings Per Week/Day:		
1 egg, 3 oz of meat/fish/poultry, 15 nuts, 1 cup beans							Fat	
							Total	

Dairy Products (2-3 servings)						Servings Per Week/Day:		
1 cup milk, 1 oz cheese, 1 cup yogurt							Fat	
							Total	

Fats, Oil, Butters (Sparingly)						Servings Per Week/Day:		
1 Tbsp for oils, dressings, mayo, nut butters and butter/margarine							Fat	
							Total	

Sweets & Snacks (Sparingly)						Servings Per Week/Day:		
1 piece of candy, 1 serving of fast food, 1 serving of snack foods							Fat	
							Total	

Beverages/Water (8-10 cups)						Servings Per Week/Day:		
1 cup of water (Track your soda, coffee, tea, & alcohol calories here)								
							Total	

Difference: _____   Total Calories: _____

Supplements

Mood and Complexion

Mood		Complexion	
Notes:			

Exercise Page - Week Five - Day 4

Date: _____   Calories Burned: _____

Remember to warm up prior to exercising!

Cardio Training			Strength Training	
Time	Distance	Cal Burn	Time	Increases

Muscle Group	Weight	Repetitions
Upper Body Exercises		
Neck		
Delts (upper arm)		
Traps (Upper back)		
Pecs (chest)		
Biceps (front arm)		
Triceps (back arm)		
Oblique (waist)		
Abs (stomach)		
Lats (middle back)		
Lower Body Exercises		
Lower Back		
Inner Thigh		
Outer Thigh		
Quads (front thigh)		
Gluts (buttocks)		
Hamstring (back thigh)		
Calves (lower back leg)		
Push-ups		
Sit-ups		
Lunges		
Squats		

Diet Page - Week Five - Day 5

Calorie Intake Required: _____   Date: _____

Fruits (2-4 Servings)					Servings Per Week/Day:			
1 piece, 1/2 cup canned, 1 oz dried, 6 oz juice					**Fat Calories**			
							Total	

Vegetables (3-5 Servings)					Servings Per Week/Day:			
1 piece, 1 cup raw, 1/2 cup canned, 1 oz dried, 6 oz juice						**Fat**		
							Total	

Whole Grains (6-11 servings)					Servings Per Week/Day:			
1 slice bread, 1/2 muffin/bun/bagel/tortilla, 1/2 c. pasta/rice, 1oz b/fast cereal						**Fat**		
							Total	

Meats, Beans, Eggs (2-3 Servings)					Servings Per Week/Day:			
1 egg, 3 oz of meat/fish/poultry, 15 nuts, 1 cup beans						**Fat**		
							Total	

Dairy Products (2-3 servings)					Servings Per Week/Day:			
1 cup milk, 1 oz cheese, 1 cup yogurt						**Fat**		
							Total	

Fats, Oil, Butters (Sparingly)					Servings Per Week/Day:			
1 Tbsp for oils, dressings, mayo, nut butters and butter/margarine						**Fat**		
							Total	

Sweets & Snacks (Sparingly)					Servings Per Week/Day:			
1 piece of candy, 1 serving of fast food, 1 serving of snack foods						**Fat**		
							Total	

Beverages/Water (8-10 cups)					Servings Per Week/Day:			
1 cup of water (Track your soda, coffee, tea, & alcohol calories here)								
							Total	

Difference: _____   Total Calories: _____

Supplements

Mood and Complexion

Mood		Complexion	
Notes:			

Exercise Page - Week Five - Day 5

Date: _____   Calories Burned: _____

Remember to warm up prior to exercising!

Cardio Training			Strength Training	
Time	Distance	Cal Burn	Time	Increases

Muscle Group	Weight	Repetitions
Upper Body Exercises		
Neck		
Delts (upper arm)		
Traps (Upper back)		
Pecs (chest)		
Biceps (front arm)		
Triceps (back arm)		
Oblique (waist)		
Abs (stomach)		
Lats (middle back)		
Lower Body Exercises		
Lower Back		
Inner Thigh		
Outer Thigh		
Quads (front thigh)		
Gluts (buttocks)		
Hamstring (back thigh)		
Calves (lower back leg)		
Push-ups		
Sit-ups		
Lunges		
Squats		

Diet Page - Week Five - Day 6

Calorie Intake Required: _____ Date: _____

Fruits (2-4 Servings)					Servings Per Week/Day:		
1 piece, 1/2 cup canned, 1 oz dried, 6 oz juice					Fat Calories		
						Total	

Vegetables (3-5 Servings)					Servings Per Week/Day:		
1 piece, 1 cup raw, 1/2 cup canned, 1 oz dried, 6 oz juice						Fat	
						Total	

Whole Grains (6-11 servings)					Servings Per Week/Day:		
1 slice bread, 1/2 muffin/bun/bagel/tortilla, 1/2 c. pasta/rice, 1oz b/fast cereal						Fat	
						Total	

Meats, Beans, Eggs (2-3 Servings)					Servings Per Week/Day:		
1 egg, 3 oz of meat/fish/poultry, 15 nuts, 1 cup beans						Fat	
						Total	

Dairy Products (2-3 servings)					Servings Per Week/Day:		
1 cup milk, 1 oz cheese, 1 cup yogurt						Fat	
						Total	

Fats, Oil, Butters (Sparingly)					Servings Per Week/Day:		
1 Tbsp for oils, dressings, mayo, nut butters and butter/margarine						Fat	
						Total	

Sweets & Snacks (Sparingly)					Servings Per Week/Day:		
1 piece of candy, 1 serving of fast food, 1 serving of snack foods						Fat	
						Total	

Beverages/Water (8-10 cups)					Servings Per Week/Day:		
1 cup of water (Track your soda, coffee, tea, & alcohol calories here)							
						Total	

Difference: _____   Total Calories: _____

Supplements

Mood and Complexion

Mood		Complexion	
Notes:			

Exercise Page - Week Five - Day 6

Date: _____   Calories Burned: _____

Remember to warm up prior to exercising!

Cardio Training			Strength Training	
Time	Distance	Cal Burn	Time	Increases

Muscle Group	Weight	Repetitions
Upper Body Exercises		
Neck		
Delts (upper arm)		
Traps (Upper back)		
Pecs (chest)		
Biceps (front arm)		
Triceps (back arm)		
Oblique (waist)		
Abs (stomach)		
Lats (middle back)		
Lower Body Exercises		
Lower Back		
Inner Thigh		
Outer Thigh		
Quads (front thigh)		
Gluts (buttocks)		
Hamstring (back thigh)		
Calves (lower back leg)		
Push-ups		
Sit ups		
Lunges		
Squats		

Diet Page - Week Five - Day 7

Calorie Intake Required: _____   Date: _____

Fruits (2-4 Servings)						Servings Per Week/Day:	
1 piece, 1/2 cup canned, 1 oz dried, 6 oz juice						Fat Calories	
						Total	

Vegetables (3-5 Servings)						Servings Per Week/Day:	
1 piece, 1 cup raw, 1/2 cup canned, 1 oz dried, 6 oz juice						Fat	
						Total	

Whole Grains (6-11 servings)						Servings Per Week/Day:	
1 slice bread, 1/2 muffin/bun/bagel/tortilla, 1/2 c. pasta/rice, 1oz b/fast cereal						Fat	
						Total	

Meats, Beans, Eggs (2-3 Servings)						Servings Per Week/Day:	
1 egg, 3 oz of meat/fish/poultry, 15 nuts, 1 cup beans						Fat	
						Total	

Dairy Products (2-3 servings)						Servings Per Week/Day:	
1 cup milk, 1 oz cheese, 1 cup yogurt						Fat	
						Total	

Fats, Oil, Butters (Sparingly)						Servings Per Week/Day:	
1 Tbsp for oils, dressings, mayo, nut butters and butter/margarine						Fat	
						Total	

Sweets & Snacks (Sparingly)						Servings Per Week/Day:	
1 piece of candy, 1 serving of fast food, 1 serving of snack foods						Fat	
						Total	

Beverages/Water (8-10 cups)						Servings Per Week/Day:	
1 cup of water (Track your soda, coffee, tea, & alcohol calories here)							
						Total	

Difference: _____   Total Calories: _____

Supplements

Mood and Complexion

Mood		Complexion	
Notes:			

Exercise Page - Week Five - Day 7

Date: _____　　　Calories Burned: _____

Remember to warm up prior to exercising!

Cardio Training			Strength Training	
Time	Distance	Cal Burn	Time	Increases

Muscle Group	Weight	Repetitions
Upper Body Exercises		
Neck		
Delts (upper arm)		
Traps (Upper back)		
Pecs (chest)		
Biceps (front arm)		
Triceps (back arm)		
Oblique (waist)		
Abs (stomach)		
Lats (middle back)		
Lower Body Exercises		
Lower Back		
Inner Thigh		
Outer Thigh		
Quads (front thigh)		
Gluts (buttocks)		
Hamstring (back thigh)		
Calves (lower back leg)		
Push-ups		
Sit-ups		
Lunges		
Squats		

Notes:

Day Of Week	Intake Calories	Burned Calories
Sunday		
Monday		
Tuesday		
Wednesday		
Thursday		
Friday		
Saturday		
Totals		

Tracking Pages
Week Six

Did you ...

- Write your measurements on the Progress Chart?
- Recalculate your formulas from the diet tips section if you're counting calories?

You should be in the routine of choosing your foods from a variety of sources, and exercising on a regular basis. You should also be noticing a lot of changes in your body.

Write your changes below:

Diet Page - Week Six - Day 1

Calorie Intake Required: _____   Date: _____

Fruits (2-4 Servings)						Servings Per Week/Day:		
1 piece, 1/2 cup canned, 1 oz dried, 6 oz juice						**Fat Calories**		
							Total	

Vegetables (3-5 Servings)						Servings Per Week/Day:		
1 piece, 1 cup raw, 1/2 cup canned, 1 oz dried, 6 oz juice							**Fat**	
							Total	

Whole Grains (6-11 servings)						Servings Per Week/Day:		
1 slice bread, 1/2 muffin/bun/bagel/tortilla, 1/2 c. pasta/rice, 1oz b/fast cereal							**Fat**	
							Total	

Meats, Beans, Eggs (2-3 Servings)						Servings Per Week/Day:		
1 egg, 3 oz of meat/fish/poultry, 15 nuts, 1 cup beans							**Fat**	
							Total	

Dairy Products (2-3 servings)						Servings Per Week/Day:		
1 cup milk, 1 oz cheese, 1 cup yogurt							**Fat**	
							Total	

Fats, Oil, Butters (Sparingly)						Servings Per Week/Day:		
1 Tbsp for oils, dressings, mayo, nut butters and butter/margarine							**Fat**	
							Total	

Sweets & Snacks (Sparingly)						Servings Per Week/Day:		
1 piece of candy, 1 serving of fast food, 1 serving of snack foods							**Fat**	
							Total	

Beverages/Water (8-10 cups)						Servings Per Week/Day:		
1 cup of water (Track your soda, coffee, tea, & alcohol calories here)								
							Total	

Difference: _____   Total Calories: _____

Supplements

Mood and Complexion

Mood		Complexion	
Notes:			

Exercise Page - Week Six - Day 1

Date: _____   Calories Burned: _____

Remember to warm up prior to exercising!

Cardio Training			Strength Training	
Time	Distance	Cal Burn	Time	Increases

Muscle Group	Weight	Repetitions
Upper Body Exercises		
Neck		
Delts (upper arm)		
Traps (Upper back)		
Pecs (chest)		
Biceps (front arm)		
Triceps (back arm)		
Oblique (waist)		
Abs (stomach)		
Lats (middle back)		
Lower Body Exercises		
Lower Back		
Inner Thigh		
Outer Thigh		
Quads (front thigh)		
Gluts (buttocks)		
Hamstring (back thigh)		
Calves (lower back leg)		
Push-ups		
Sit-ups		
Lunges		
Squats		

Diet Page - Week Six - Day 2

Calorie Intake Required: _____   Date: _____

Fruits (2-4 Servings)								Servings Per Week/Day:		
1 piece, 1/2 cup canned, 1 oz dried, 6 oz juice								**Fat Calories**		
									Total	

Vegetables (3-5 Servings)								Servings Per Week/Day:		
1 piece, 1 cup raw, 1/2 cup canned, 1 oz dried, 6 oz juice									**Fat**	
									Total	

Whole Grains (6-11 servings)								Servings Per Week/Day:		
1 slice bread, 1/2 muffin/bun/bagel/tortilla, 1/2 c. pasta/rice, 1oz b/fast cereal									**Fat**	
									Total	

Meats, Beans, Eggs (2-3 Servings)								Servings Per Week/Day:		
1 egg, 3 oz of meat/fish/poultry, 15 nuts, 1 cup beans									**Fat**	
									Total	

Dairy Products (2-3 servings)								Servings Per Week/Day:		
1 cup milk, 1 oz cheese, 1 cup yogurt									**Fat**	
									Total	

Fats, Oil, Butters (Sparingly)								Servings Per Week/Day:		
1 Tbsp for oils, dressings, mayo, nut butters and butter/margarine									**Fat**	
									Total	

Sweets & Snacks (Sparingly)								Servings Per Week/Day:		
1 piece of candy, 1 serving of fast food, 1 serving of snack foods									**Fat**	
									Total	

Beverages/Water (8-10 cups)								Servings Per Week/Day:		
1 cup of water (Track your soda, coffee, tea, & alcohol calories here)										
									Total	

Difference: _____   Total Calories: _____

Supplements

Mood and Complexion

Mood		Complexion	
Notes:			

Exercise Page - Week Six - Day 2

Date: _____   Calories Burned: _____

Remember to warm up prior to exercising!

Cardio Training			Strength Training	
Time	Distance	Cal Burn	Time	Increases

Muscle Group	Weight	Repetitions
Upper Body Exercises		
Neck		
Delts (upper arm)		
Traps (Upper back)		
Pecs (chest)		
Biceps (front arm)		
Triceps (back arm)		
Oblique (waist)		
Abs (stomach)		
Lats (middle back)		
Lower Body Exercises		
Lower Back		
Inner Thigh		
Outer Thigh		
Quads (front thigh)		
Gluts (buttocks)		
Hamstring (back thigh)		
Calves (lower back leg)		
Push-ups		
Sit-ups		
Lunges		
Squats		

Diet Page - Week Six - Day 3

Calorie Intake Required: _____   Date: _____

Fruits (2-4 Servings)						Servings Per Week/Day:			
1 piece, 1/2 cup canned, 1 oz dried, 6 oz juice						Fat Calories			
								Total	

Vegetables (3-5 Servings)						Servings Per Week/Day:			
1 piece, 1 cup raw, 1/2 cup canned, 1 oz dried, 6 oz juice							Fat		
								Total	

Whole Grains (6-11 servings)						Servings Per Week/Day:			
1 slice bread, 1/2 muffin/bun/bagel/tortilla, 1/2 c. pasta/rice, 1oz b/fast cereal							Fat		
								Total	

Meats, Beans, Eggs (2-3 Servings)						Servings Per Week/Day:			
1 egg, 3 oz of meat/fish/poultry, 15 nuts, 1 cup beans							Fat		
								Total	

Dairy Products (2-3 servings)						Servings Per Week/Day:			
1 cup milk, 1 oz cheese, 1 cup yogurt							Fat		
								Total	

Fats, Oil, Butters (Sparingly)						Servings Per Week/Day:			
1 Tbsp for oils, dressings, mayo, nut butters and butter/margarine							Fat		
								Total	

Sweets & Snacks (Sparingly)						Servings Per Week/Day:			
1 piece of candy, 1 serving of fast food, 1 serving of snack foods							Fat		
								Total	

Beverages/Water (8-10 cups)						Servings Per Week/Day:			
1 cup of water (Track your soda, coffee, tea, & alcohol calories here)									
								Total	

Difference: _____   Total Calories: _____

Supplements

Mood and Complexion

Mood		Complexion	
Notes:			

Exercise Page - Week Six - Day 3

Date: _____   Calories Burned: _____

Remember to warm up prior to exercising!

Cardio Training			Strength Training	
Time	Distance	Cal Burn	Time	Increases

Muscle Group	Weight	Repetitions
Upper Body Exercises		
Neck		
Delts (upper arm)		
Traps (Upper back)		
Pecs (chest)		
Biceps (front arm)		
Triceps (back arm)		
Oblique (waist)		
Abs (stomach)		
Lats (middle back)		
Lower Body Exercises		
Lower Back		
Inner Thigh		
Outer Thigh		
Quads (front thigh)		
Gluts (buttocks)		
Hamstring (back thigh)		
Calves (lower back leg)		
Push-ups		
Sit-ups		
Lunges		
Squats		

Diet Page - Week Six - Day 4

Calorie Intake Required: _____   Date: _____

Fruits (2-4 Servings)						Servings Per Week/Day:			
1 piece, 1/2 cup canned, 1 oz dried, 6 oz juice						Fat Calories			
								Total	

Vegetables (3-5 Servings)						Servings Per Week/Day:			
1 piece, 1 cup raw, 1/2 cup canned, 1 oz dried, 6 oz juice								Fat	
								Total	

Whole Grains (6-11 servings)						Servings Per Week/Day:			
1 slice bread, 1/2 muffin/bun/bagel/tortilla, 1/2 c. pasta/rice, 1oz b/fast cereal								Fat	
								Total	

Meats, Beans, Eggs (2-3 Servings)						Servings Per Week/Day:			
1 egg, 3 oz of meat/fish/poultry, 15 nuts, 1 cup beans								Fat	
								Total	

Dairy Products (2-3 servings)						Servings Per Week/Day:			
1 cup milk, 1 oz cheese, 1 cup yogurt								Fat	
								Total	

Fats, Oil, Butters (Sparingly)						Servings Per Week/Day:			
1 Tbsp for oils, dressings, mayo, nut butters and butter/margarine								Fat	
								Total	

Sweets & Snacks (Sparingly)						Servings Per Week/Day:			
1 piece of candy, 1 serving of fast food, 1 serving of snack foods								Fat	
								Total	

Beverages/Water (8-10 cups)						Servings Per Week/Day:			
1 cup of water (Track your soda, coffee, tea, & alcohol calories here)									
								Total	

Difference: _____   Total Calories: _____

Supplements

Mood and Complexion

Mood		Complexion	
Notes:			

Exercise Page - Week Six - Day 4

Date: _____   Calories Burned: _____

Remember to warm up prior to exercising!

Cardio Training			Strength Training	
Time	Distance	Cal Burn	Time	Increases

Muscle Group	Weight	Repetitions
Upper Body Exercises		
Neck		
Delts (upper arm)		
Traps (Upper back)		
Pecs (chest)		
Biceps (front arm)		
Triceps (back arm)		
Oblique (waist)		
Abs (stomach)		
Lats (middle back)		
Lower Body Exercises		
Lower Back		
Inner Thigh		
Outer Thigh		
Quads (front thigh)		
Gluts (buttocks)		
Hamstring (back thigh)		
Calves (lower back leg)		
Push-ups		
Sit-ups		
Lunges		
Squats		

Diet Page - Week Six - Day 5

Calorie Intake Required: _____   Date: _____

Fruits (2-4 Servings)						Servings Per Week/Day:		
1 piece, 1/2 cup canned, 1 oz dried, 6 oz juice						**Fat Calories**		
							Total	

Vegetables (3-5 Servings)						Servings Per Week/Day:		
1 piece, 1 cup raw, 1/2 cup canned, 1 oz dried, 6 oz juice							**Fat**	
							Total	

Whole Grains (6-11 servings)						Servings Per Week/Day:		
1 slice bread, 1/2 muffin/bun/bagel/tortilla, 1/2 c. pasta/rice, 1oz b/fast cereal							**Fat**	
							Total	

Meats, Beans, Eggs (2-3 Servings)						Servings Per Week/Day:		
1 egg, 3 oz of meat/fish/poultry, 15 nuts, 1 cup beans							**Fat**	
							Total	

Dairy Products (2-3 servings)						Servings Per Week/Day:		
1 cup milk, 1 oz cheese, 1 cup yogurt							**Fat**	
							Total	

Fats, Oil, Butters (Sparingly)						Servings Per Week/Day:		
1 Tbsp for oils, dressings, mayo, nut butters and butter/margarine							**Fat**	
							Total	

Sweets & Snacks (Sparingly)						Servings Per Week/Day:		
1 piece of candy, 1 serving of fast food, 1 serving of snack foods							**Fat**	
							Total	

Beverages/Water (8-10 cups)						Servings Per Week/Day:		
1 cup of water (Track your soda, coffee, tea, & alcohol calories here)								
							Total	

Difference: _____   Total Calories: _____

Supplements

Mood and Complexion

Mood		Complexion	
Notes:			

Exercise Page - Week Six - Day 5

Date: _____   Calories Burned: _____

Remember to warm up prior to exercising!

Cardio Training			Strength Training	
Time	Distance	Cal Burn	Time	Increases

Muscle Group	Weight	Repetitions
Upper Body Exercises		
Neck		
Delts (upper arm)		
Traps (Upper back)		
Pecs (chest)		
Biceps (front arm)		
Triceps (back arm)		
Oblique (waist)		
Abs (stomach)		
Lats (middle back)		
Lower Body Exercises		
Lower Back		
Inner Thigh		
Outer Thigh		
Quads (front thigh)		
Gluts (buttocks)		
Hamstring (back thigh)		
Calves (lower back leg)		
Push-ups		
Sit-ups		
Lunges		
Squats		

Diet Page - Week Six - Day 6

Calorie Intake Required: _____ Date: _____

Fruits (2-4 Servings)					Servings Per Week/Day:		
1 piece, 1/2 cup canned, 1 oz dried, 6 oz juice					Fat Calories		
						Total	

Vegetables (3-5 Servings)					Servings Per Week/Day:		
1 piece, 1 cup raw, 1/2 cup canned, 1 oz dried, 6 oz juice						Fat	
						Total	

Whole Grains (6-11 servings)					Servings Per Week/Day:		
1 slice bread, 1/2 muffin/bun/bagel/tortilla, 1/2 c. pasta/rice, 1oz b/fast cereal						Fat	
						Total	

Meats, Beans, Eggs (2-3 Servings)					Servings Per Week/Day:		
1 egg, 3 oz of meat/fish/poultry, 15 nuts, 1 cup beans						Fat	
						Total	

Dairy Products (2-3 servings)					Servings Per Week/Day:		
1 cup milk, 1 oz cheese, 1 cup yogurt						Fat	
						Total	

Fats, Oil, Butters (Sparingly)					Servings Per Week/Day:		
1 Tbsp for oils, dressings, mayo, nut butters and butter/margarine						Fat	
						Total	

Sweets & Snacks (Sparingly)					Servings Per Week/Day:		
1 piece of candy, 1 serving of fast food, 1 serving of snack foods						Fat	
						Total	

Beverages/Water (8-10 cups)					Servings Per Week/Day:		
1 cup of water (Track your soda, coffee, tea, & alcohol calories here)							
						Total	

Difference: _____   Total Calories: _____

Supplements

Mood and Complexion

Mood		Complexion	
Notes:			

Exercise Page - Week Six - Day 6

Date: _____   Calories Burned: _____

Remember to warm up prior to exercising!

Cardio Training			Strength Training	
Time	Distance	Cal Burn	Time	Increases

Muscle Group	Weight	Repetitions
Upper Body Exercises		
Neck		
Delts (upper arm)		
Traps (Upper back)		
Pecs (chest)		
Biceps (front arm)		
Triceps (back arm)		
Oblique (waist)		
Abs (stomach)		
Lats (middle back)		
Lower Body Exercises		
Lower Back		
Inner Thigh		
Outer Thigh		
Quads (front thigh)		
Gluts (buttocks)		
Hamstring (back thigh)		
Calves (lower back leg)		
Push-ups		
Sit-ups		
Lunges		
Squats		

Diet Page - Week Six - Day 7

Calorie Intake Required: _____   Date: _____

Fruits (2-4 Servings)						Servings Per Week/Day:		
1 piece, 1/2 cup canned, 1 oz dried, 6 oz juice						Fat Calories		
								Total

Vegetables (3-5 Servings)						Servings Per Week/Day:		
1 piece, 1 cup raw, 1/2 cup canned, 1 oz dried, 6 oz juice							Fat	
								Total

Whole Grains (6-11 servings)						Servings Per Week/Day:		
1 slice bread, 1/2 muffin/bun/bagel/tortilla, 1/2 c. pasta/rice, 1oz b/fast cereal							Fat	
								Total

Meats, Beans, Eggs (2-3 Servings)						Servings Per Week/Day:		
1 egg, 3 oz of meat/fish/poultry, 15 nuts, 1 cup beans							Fat	
								Total

Dairy Products (2-3 servings)						Servings Per Week/Day:		
1 cup milk, 1 oz cheese, 1 cup yogurt							Fat	
								Total

Fats, Oil, Butters (Sparingly)						Servings Per Week/Day:		
1 Tbsp for oils, dressings, mayo, nut butters and butter/margarine							Fat	
								Total

Sweets & Snacks (Sparingly)						Servings Per Week/Day:		
1 piece of candy, 1 serving of fast food, 1 serving of snack foods							Fat	
								Total

Beverages/Water (8-10 cups)						Servings Per Week/Day:		
1 cup of water (Track your soda, coffee, tea, & alcohol calories here)								
								Total

Difference: _____   Total Calories: _____

Supplements

Mood and Complexion

Mood		Complexion	
Notes:			

Exercise Page - Week Six - Day 7

Date: _____   Calories Burned: _____

Remember to warm up prior to exercising!

Cardio Training			Strength Training	
Time	Distance	Cal Burn	Time	Increases

Muscle Group	Weight	Repetitions
Upper Body Exercises		
Neck		
Delts (upper arm)		
Traps (Upper back)		
Pecs (chest)		
Biceps (front arm)		
Triceps (back arm)		
Oblique (waist)		
Abs (stomach)		
Lats (middle back)		
Lower Body Exercises		
Lower Back		
Inner Thigh		
Outer Thigh		
Quads (front thigh)		
Gluts (buttocks)		
Hamstring (back thigh)		
Calves (lower back leg)		
Push-ups		
Sit-ups		
Lunges		
Squats		

Formula Page   Date: _____

Use this page to recalculate when you've lost weight!

_____ X _____ = _____
Current Weight   Activity Multiplier   Calories Required for this weight

_____ X _____ = _____
Healthy Weight   Activity Multiplier   Calories Required for this weight

_____
Difference

3500/_____ = _____
      Difference   Days to lose 1 pound of body fat

To recalculate with exercising:

_____ X 7 = _____ calories reduced per week
Difference

_____ X _____ = _____ extra calories burned per week
Activity   Days per week

_____ + _____ = _____ / 7 = _____
Reduced Calories   Extra Calories Burned   Total for the Week   avg reduced per day

3500/_____ = _____
      Avg reduced per day   Days to lose 1 pound of body fat

Notes:

Day Of Week	Intake Calories	Burned Calories
Sunday		
Monday		
Tuesday		
Wednesday		
Thursday		
Friday		
Saturday		
Totals		

Tracking Pages
Week Seven

Did you ...

- Write your measurements on the Progress Chart?

Write your changes here:

Diet Page - Week Seven - Day 1

Calorie Intake Required: _____   Date: _____

Fruits (2-4 Servings)							Servings Per Week/Day:		
1 piece, 1/2 cup canned, 1 oz dried, 6 oz juice							Fat Calories		
								Total	

Vegetables (3-5 Servings)							Servings Per Week/Day:		
1 piece, 1 cup raw, 1/2 cup canned, 1 oz dried, 6 oz juice								Fat	
								Total	

Whole Grains (6-11 servings)							Servings Per Week/Day:		
1 slice bread, 1/2 muffin/bun/bagel/tortilla, 1/2 c. pasta/rice, 1oz b/fast cereal								Fat	
								Total	

Meats, Beans, Eggs (2-3 Servings)							Servings Per Week/Day:		
1 egg, 3 oz of meat/fish/poultry, 15 nuts, 1 cup beans								Fat	
								Total	

Dairy Products (2-3 servings)							Servings Per Week/Day:		
1 cup milk, 1 oz cheese, 1 cup yogurt								Fat	
								Total	

Fats, Oil, Butters (Sparingly)							Servings Per Week/Day:		
1 Tbsp for oils, dressings, mayo, nut butters and butter/margarine								Fat	
								Total	

Sweets & Snacks (Sparingly)							Servings Per Week/Day:		
1 piece of candy, 1 serving of fast food, 1 serving of snack foods								Fat	
								Total	

Beverages/Water (8-10 cups)							Servings Per Week/Day:		
1 cup of water (Track your soda, coffee, tea, & alcohol calories here)									
								Total	

Difference: _____   Total Calories: _____

Supplements

Mood and Complexion

Mood		Complexion	
Notes:			

Exercise Page - Week Seven - Day 1

Date: _____   Calories Burned: _____

Remember to warm up prior to exercising!

Cardio Training			Strength Training	
Time	Distance	Cal Burn	Time	Increases

Muscle Group	Weight	Repetitions
Upper Body Exercises		
Neck		
Delts (upper arm)		
Traps (Upper back)		
Pecs (chest)		
Biceps (front arm)		
Triceps (back arm)		
Oblique (waist)		
Abs (stomach)		
Lats (middle back)		
Lower Body Exercises		
Lower Back		
Inner Thigh		
Outer Thigh		
Quads (front thigh)		
Gluts (buttocks)		
Hamstring (back thigh)		
Calves (lower back leg)		
Push-ups		
Sit-ups		
Lunges		
Squats		

Diet Page - Week Seven - Day 2

Calorie Intake Required: _____ Date: _____

Fruits (2-4 Servings)
Servings Per Week/Day:

1 piece, 1/2 cup canned, 1 oz dried, 6 oz juice	Fat Calories							
							Total	

Vegetables (3-5 Servings)
Servings Per Week/Day:

1 piece, 1 cup raw, 1/2 cup canned, 1 oz dried, 6 oz juice						Fat	
						Total	

Whole Grains (6-11 servings)
Servings Per Week/Day:

1 slice bread, 1/2 muffin/bun/bagel/tortilla, 1/2 c. pasta/rice, 1oz b/fast cereal						Fat	
						Total	

Meats, Beans, Eggs (2-3 Servings)
Servings Per Week/Day:

1 egg, 3 oz of meat/fish/poultry, 15 nuts, 1 cup beans						Fat	
						Total	

Dairy Products (2-3 servings)
Servings Per Week/Day:

1 cup milk, 1 oz cheese, 1 cup yogurt						Fat	
						Total	

Fats, Oil, Butters (Sparingly)
Servings Per Week/Day:

1 Tbsp for oils, dressings, mayo, nut butters and butter/margarine						Fat	
						Total	

Sweets & Snacks (Sparingly)
Servings Per Week/Day:

1 piece of candy, 1 serving of fast food, 1 serving of snack foods						Fat	
						Total	

Beverages/Water (8-10 cups)
Servings Per Week/Day:

1 cup of water (Track your soda, coffee, tea, & alcohol calories here)							
						Total	

Difference: _____   Total Calories: _____

Supplements

Mood and Complexion

Mood		Complexion	
Notes:			

Exercise Page - Week Seven - Day 2

Date: _____　　　Calories Burned: _____

Remember to warm up prior to exercising!

Cardio Training			Strength Training	
Time	Distance	Cal Burn	Time	Increases

Muscle Group	Weight	Repetitions
Upper Body Exercises		
Neck		
Delts (upper arm)		
Traps (Upper back)		
Pecs (chest)		
Biceps (front arm)		
Triceps (back arm)		
Oblique (waist)		
Abs (stomach)		
Lats (middle back)		
Lower Body Exercises		
Lower Back		
Inner Thigh		
Outer Thigh		
Quads (front thigh)		
Gluts (buttocks)		
Hamstring (back thigh)		
Calves (lower back leg)		
Push-ups		
Sit-ups		
Lunges		
Squats		

Diet Page - Week Seven - Day 3

Calorie Intake Required: _____   Date: _____

Fruits (2-4 Servings)					Servings Per Week/Day:				
1 piece, 1/2 cup canned, 1 oz dried, 6 oz juice					Fat Calories				
								Total	

Vegetables (3-5 Servings)					Servings Per Week/Day:				
1 piece, 1 cup raw, 1/2 cup canned, 1 oz dried, 6 oz juice								Fat	
								Total	

Whole Grains (6-11 servings)					Servings Per Week/Day:				
1 slice bread, 1/2 muffin/bun/bagel/tortilla, 1/2 c. pasta/rice, 1oz b/fast cereal								Fat	
								Total	

Meats, Beans, Eggs (2-3 Servings)					Servings Per Week/Day:				
1 egg, 3 oz of meat/fish/poultry, 15 nuts, 1 cup beans								Fat	
								Total	

Dairy Products (2-3 servings)					Servings Per Week/Day:				
1 cup milk, 1 oz cheese, 1 cup yogurt								Fat	
								Total	

Fats, Oil, Butters (Sparingly)					Servings Per Week/Day:				
1 Tbsp for oils, dressings, mayo, nut butters and butter/margarine								Fat	
								Total	

Sweets & Snacks (Sparingly)					Servings Per Week/Day:				
1 piece of candy, 1 serving of fast food, 1 serving of snack foods								Fat	
								Total	

Beverages/Water (8-10 cups)					Servings Per Week/Day:				
1 cup of water (Track your soda, coffee, tea, & alcohol calories here)									
								Total	

Difference: _____   Total Calories: _____

Supplements

Mood and Complexion

Mood		Complexion	
Notes:			

Exercise Page - Week Seven - Day 3

Date: _____   Calories Burned: _____

Remember to warm up prior to exercising!

Cardio Training			Strength Training	
Time	Distance	Cal Burn	Time	Increases

Muscle Group	Weight	Repetitions
Upper Body Exercises		
Neck		
Delts (upper arm)		
Traps (Upper back)		
Pecs (chest)		
Biceps (front arm)		
Triceps (back arm)		
Oblique (waist)		
Abs (stomach)		
Lats (middle back)		
Lower Body Exercises		
Lower Back		
Inner Thigh		
Outer Thigh		
Quads (front thigh)		
Gluts (buttocks)		
Hamstring (back thigh)		
Calves (lower back leg)		
Push-ups		
Sit-ups		
Lunges		
Squats		

Diet Page - Week Seven - Day 4

Calorie Intake Required: _____   Date: _____

Fruits (2-4 Servings)							Servings Per Week/Day:			
1 piece, 1/2 cup canned, 1 oz dried, 6 oz juice							**Fat Calories**			
									Total	

Vegetables (3-5 Servings)							Servings Per Week/Day:		
1 piece, 1 cup raw, 1/2 cup canned, 1 oz dried, 6 oz juice								**Fat**	
								Total	

Whole Grains (6-11 servings)							Servings Per Week/Day:		
1 slice bread, 1/2 muffin/bun/bagel/tortilla, 1/2 c. pasta/rice, 1oz b/fast cereal								**Fat**	
								Total	

Meats, Beans, Eggs (2-3 Servings)						Servings Per Week/Day:		
1 egg, 3 oz of meat/fish/poultry, 15 nuts, 1 cup beans							**Fat**	
							Total	

Dairy Products (2-3 servings)						Servings Per Week/Day:		
1 cup milk, 1 oz cheese, 1 cup yogurt							**Fat**	
							Total	

Fats, Oil, Butters (Sparingly)						Servings Per Week/Day:		
1 Tbsp for oils, dressings, mayo, nut butters and butter/margarine							**Fat**	
							Total	

Sweets & Snacks (Sparingly)						Servings Per Week/Day:		
1 piece of candy, 1 serving of fast food, 1 serving of snack foods							**Fat**	
							Total	

Beverages/Water (8-10 cups)						Servings Per Week/Day:		
1 cup of water (Track your soda, coffee, tea, & alcohol calories here)								
							Total	

Difference: _____   Total Calories: _____

Supplements

Mood and Complexion

Mood		Complexion	
Notes:			

Exercise Page - Week Seven - Day 4

Date: _____   Calories Burned: _____

Remember to warm up prior to exercising!

Cardio Training			Strength Training	
Time	Distance	Cal Burn	Time	Increases

Muscle Group	Weight	Repetitions
Upper Body Exercises		
Neck		
Delts (upper arm)		
Traps (Upper back)		
Pecs (chest)		
Biceps (front arm)		
Triceps (back arm)		
Oblique (waist)		
Abs (stomach)		
Lats (middle back)		
Lower Body Exercises		
Lower Back		
Inner Thigh		
Outer Thigh		
Quads (front thigh)		
Gluts (buttocks)		
Hamstring (back thigh)		
Calves (lower back leg)		
Push-ups		
Sit-ups		
Lunges		
Squats		

Diet Page - Week Seven - Day 5

Calorie Intake Required: _____   Date: _____

Fruits (2-4 Servings)						Servings Per Week/Day:		
1 piece, 1/2 cup canned, 1 oz dried, 6 oz juice						Fat Calories		
							Total	

Vegetables (3-5 Servings)						Servings Per Week/Day:		
1 piece, 1 cup raw, 1/2 cup canned, 1 oz dried, 6 oz juice							Fat	
							Total	

Whole Grains (6-11 servings)						Servings Per Week/Day:		
1 slice bread, 1/2 muffin/bun/bagel/tortilla, 1/2 c. pasta/rice, 1oz b/fast cereal							Fat	
							Total	

Meats, Beans, Eggs (2-3 Servings)						Servings Per Week/Day:		
1 egg, 3 oz of meat/fish/poultry, 15 nuts, 1 cup beans							Fat	
							Total	

Dairy Products (2-3 servings)						Servings Per Week/Day:		
1 cup milk, 1 oz cheese, 1 cup yogurt							Fat	
							Total	

Fats, Oil, Butters (Sparingly)						Servings Per Week/Day:		
1 Tbsp for oils, dressings, mayo, nut butters and butter/margarine							Fat	
							Total	

Sweets & Snacks (Sparingly)						Servings Per Week/Day:		
1 piece of candy, 1 serving of fast food, 1 serving of snack foods							Fat	
							Total	

Beverages/Water (8-10 cups)						Servings Per Week/Day:		
1 cup of water (Track your soda, coffee, tea, & alcohol calories here)								
							Total	

Difference: _____   Total Calories: _____

Supplements

Mood and Complexion

Mood		Complexion	
Notes:			

Exercise Page - Week Seven - Day 5

Date: _____   Calories Burned: _____

Remember to warm up prior to exercising!

Cardio Training			Strength Training	
Time	Distance	Cal Burn	Time	Increases

Muscle Group	Weight	Repetitions
Upper Body Exercises		
Neck		
Delts (upper arm)		
Traps (Upper back)		
Pecs (chest)		
Biceps (front arm)		
Triceps (back arm)		
Oblique (waist)		
Abs (stomach)		
Lats (middle back)		
Lower Body Exercises		
Lower Back		
Inner Thigh		
Outer Thigh		
Quads (front thigh)		
Gluts (buttocks)		
Hamstring (back thigh)		
Calves (lower back leg)		
Push-ups		
Sit-ups		
Lunges		
Squats		

Diet Page - Week Seven - Day 6

Calorie Intake Required: _____   Date: _____

Fruits (2-4 Servings)						Servings Per Week/Day:			
1 piece, 1/2 cup canned, 1 oz dried, 6 oz juice						Fat Calories			
								Total	

Vegetables (3-5 Servings)						Servings Per Week/Day:			
1 piece, 1 cup raw, 1/2 cup canned, 1 oz dried, 6 oz juice								Fat	
								Total	

Whole Grains (6-11 servings)						Servings Per Week/Day:			
1 slice bread, 1/2 muffin/bun/bagel/tortilla, 1/2 c. pasta/rice, 1oz b/fast cereal								Fat	
								Total	

Meats, Beans, Eggs (2-3 Servings)						Servings Per Week/Day:			
1 egg, 3 oz of meat/fish/poultry, 15 nuts, 1 cup beans								Fat	
								Total	

Dairy Products (2-3 servings)						Servings Per Week/Day:			
1 cup milk, 1 oz cheese, 1 cup yogurt								Fat	
								Total	

Fats, Oil, Butters (Sparingly)						Servings Per Week/Day:			
1 Tbsp for oils, dressings, mayo, nut butters and butter/margarine								Fat	
								Total	

Sweets & Snacks (Sparingly)						Servings Per Week/Day:			
1 piece of candy, 1 serving of fast food, 1 serving of snack foods								Fat	
								Total	

Beverages/Water (8-10 cups)						Servings Per Week/Day:			
1 cup of water (Track your soda, coffee, tea, & alcohol calories here)									
								Total	

Difference: _____   Total Calories: _____

Supplements

Mood and Complexion

Mood		Complexion	
Notes:			

Exercise Page - Week Seven - Day 6

Date: _____   Calories Burned: _____

Remember to warm up prior to exercising!

Cardio Training			Strength Training	
Time	Distance	Cal Burn	Time	Increases

Muscle Group	Weight	Repetitions
Upper Body Exercises		
Neck		
Delts (upper arm)		
Traps (Upper back)		
Pecs (chest)		
Biceps (front arm)		
Triceps (back arm)		
Oblique (waist)		
Abs (stomach)		
Lats (middle back)		
Lower Body Exercises		
Lower Back		
Inner Thigh		
Outer Thigh		
Quads (front thigh)		
Gluts (buttocks)		
Hamstring (back thigh)		
Calves (lower back leg)		
Push-ups		
Sit-ups		
Lunges		
Squats		

Diet Page - Week Seven - Day 7

Calorie Intake Required: _____   Date: _____

Fruits (2-4 Servings)						Servings Per Week/Day:			
1 piece, 1/2 cup canned, 1 oz dried, 6 oz juice						Fat Calories			
								Total	

Vegetables (3-5 Servings)						Servings Per Week/Day:			
1 piece, 1 cup raw, 1/2 cup canned, 1 oz dried, 6 oz juice							Fat		
								Total	

Whole Grains (6-11 servings)						Servings Per Week/Day:			
1 slice bread, 1/2 muffin/bun/bagel/tortilla, 1/2 c. pasta/rice, 1oz b/fast cereal							Fat		
								Total	

Meats, Beans, Eggs (2-3 Servings)						Servings Per Week/Day:			
1 egg, 3 oz of meat/fish/poultry, 15 nuts, 1 cup beans							Fat		
								Total	

Dairy Products (2-3 servings)						Servings Per Week/Day:			
1 cup milk, 1 oz cheese, 1 cup yogurt							Fat		
								Total	

Fats, Oil, Butters (Sparingly)						Servings Per Week/Day:			
1 Tbsp for oils, dressings, mayo, nut butters and butter/margarine							Fat		
								Total	

Sweets & Snacks (Sparingly)						Servings Per Week/Day:			
1 piece of candy, 1 serving of fast food, 1 serving of snack foods							Fat		
								Total	

Beverages/Water (8-10 cups)						Servings Per Week/Day:			
1 cup of water (Track your soda, coffee, tea, & alcohol calories here)									
								Total	

Difference: _____   Total Calories: _____

Supplements

Mood and Complexion

Mood		Complexion	
Notes:			

Exercise Page - Week Seven - Day 7

Date: _____   Calories Burned: _____

Remember to warm up prior to exercising!

Cardio Training			Strength Training	
Time	Distance	Cal Burn	Time	Increases

Muscle Group	Weight	Repetitions
Upper Body Exercises		
Neck		
Delts (upper arm)		
Traps (Upper back)		
Pecs (chest)		
Biceps (front arm)		
Triceps (back arm)		
Oblique (waist)		
Abs (stomach)		
Lats (middle back)		
Lower Body Exercises		
Lower Back		
Inner Thigh		
Outer Thigh		
Quads (front thigh)		
Gluts (buttocks)		
Hamstring (back thigh)		
Calves (lower back leg)		
Push-ups		
Sit-ups		
Lunges		
Squats		

Formula Page   Date: _____

Use this page to recalculate when you've lost weight!

_____ × _____ = _____
Current Weight   Activity Multiplier   Calories Required for this weight

_____ × _____ = _____
Healthy Weight   Activity Multiplier   Calories Required for this weight

_____
Difference

3500/_____ = _____
   Difference   Days to lose 1 pound of body fat

To recalculate with exercising:

_____ × 7 = _____ calories reduced per week
Difference

_____ × _____ = _____ extra calories burned per week
Activity   Days per week

_____ + _____ = _____ / 7 = _____
Reduced Calories   Extra Calories Burned   Total for the Week   avg reduced per day

3500/_____ = _____
   Avg reduced per day   Days to lose 1 pound of body fat

Notes:

Day Of Week	Intake Calories	Burned Calories
Sunday		
Monday		
Tuesday		
Wednesday		
Thursday		
Friday		
Saturday		
Totals		

Tracking Pages
Week Eight

Did you …

- Write your measurements on the Progress Chart?
- Recalculate your formulas from the diet tips section if you're counting calories?

Write your changes below:

Diet Page - Week Eight - Day 1

Calorie Intake Required: _____   Date: _____

Fruits (2-4 Servings)						Servings Per Week/Day:			
1 piece, 1/2 cup canned, 1 oz dried, 6 oz juice						Fat Calories			
								Total	

Vegetables (3-5 Servings)						Servings Per Week/Day:			
1 piece, 1 cup raw, 1/2 cup canned, 1 oz dried, 6 oz juice								Fat	
								Total	

Whole Grains (6-11 servings)						Servings Per Week/Day:			
1 slice bread, 1/2 muffin/bun/bagel/tortilla, 1/2 c. pasta/rice, 1oz b/fast cereal								Fat	
								Total	

Meats, Beans, Eggs (2-3 Servings)						Servings Per Week/Day:			
1 egg, 3 oz of meat/fish/poultry, 15 nuts, 1 cup beans								Fat	
								Total	

Dairy Products (2-3 servings)						Servings Per Week/Day:			
1 cup milk, 1 oz cheese, 1 cup yogurt								Fat	
								Total	

Fats, Oil, Butters (Sparingly)						Servings Per Week/Day:			
1 Tbsp for oils, dressings, mayo, nut butters and butter/margarine								Fat	
								Total	

Sweets & Snacks (Sparingly)						Servings Per Week/Day:			
1 piece of candy, 1 serving of fast food, 1 serving of snack foods								Fat	
								Total	

Beverages/Water (8-10 cups)						Servings Per Week/Day:			
1 cup of water (Track your soda, coffee, tea, & alcohol calories here)									
								Total	

Difference: _____   Total Calories: _____

Supplements

Mood and Complexion

Mood		Complexion	
Notes:			

Exercise Page - Week Eight - Day 1

Date: _____   Calories Burned: _____

Remember to warm up prior to exercising!

Cardio Training			Strength Training	
Time	Distance	Cal Burn	Time	Increases

Muscle Group	Weight	Repetitions
Upper Body Exercises		
Neck		
Delts (upper arm)		
Traps (Upper back)		
Pecs (chest)		
Biceps (front arm)		
Triceps (back arm)		
Oblique (waist)		
Abs (stomach)		
Lats (middle back)		
Lower Body Exercises		
Lower Back		
Inner Thigh		
Outer Thigh		
Quads (front thigh)		
Gluts (buttocks)		
Hamstring (back thigh)		
Calves (lower back leg)		
Push-ups		
Sit-ups		
Lunges		
Squats		

Diet Page - Week Eight - Day 2

Calorie Intake Required: _____ Date: _____

Fruits (2-4 Servings)							Servings Per Week/Day:		
1 piece, 1/2 cup canned, 1 oz dried, 6 oz juice							Fat Calories		
								Total	

Vegetables (3-5 Servings)							Servings Per Week/Day:		
1 piece, 1 cup raw, 1/2 cup canned, 1 oz dried, 6 oz juice								Fat	
								Total	

Whole Grains (6-11 servings)							Servings Per Week/Day:		
1 slice bread, 1/2 muffin/bun/bagel/tortilla, 1/2 c. pasta/rice, 1oz b/fast cereal								Fat	
								Total	

Meats, Beans, Eggs (2-3 Servings)							Servings Per Week/Day:		
1 egg, 3 oz of meat/fish/poultry, 15 nuts, 1 cup beans								Fat	
								Total	

Dairy Products (2-3 servings)							Servings Per Week/Day:		
1 cup milk, 1 oz cheese, 1 cup yogurt								Fat	
								Total	

Fats, Oil, Butters (Sparingly)							Servings Per Week/Day:		
1 Tbsp for oils, dressings, mayo, nut butters and butter/margarine								Fat	
								Total	

Sweets & Snacks (Sparingly)							Servings Per Week/Day:		
1 piece of candy, 1 serving of fast food, 1 serving of snack foods								Fat	
								Total	

Beverages/Water (8-10 cups)							Servings Per Week/Day:		
1 cup of water (Track your soda, coffee, tea, & alcohol calories here)									
								Total	

Difference: _____   Total Calories: _____

Supplements

Mood and Complexion

Mood		Complexion	
Notes:			

Exercise Page - Week Eight - Day 2

Date: _____   Calories Burned: _____

Remember to warm up prior to exercising!

Cardio Training			Strength Training	
Time	Distance	Cal Burn	Time	Increases

Muscle Group	Weight	Repetitions
Upper Body Exercises		
Neck		
Delts (upper arm)		
Traps (Upper back)		
Pecs (chest)		
Biceps (front arm)		
Triceps (back arm)		
Oblique (waist)		
Abs (stomach)		
Lats (middle back)		
Lower Body Exercises		
Lower Back		
Inner Thigh		
Outer Thigh		
Quads (front thigh)		
Gluts (buttocks)		
Hamstring (back thigh)		
Calves (lower back leg)		
Push-ups		
Sit-ups		
Lunges		
Squats		

Diet Page - Week Eight - Day 3

Calorie Intake Required: _____   Date: _____

Fruits (2-4 Servings)					Servings Per Week/Day:		
1 piece, 1/2 cup canned, 1 oz dried, 6 oz juice					**Fat Calories**		
						Total	

Vegetables (3-5 Servings)					Servings Per Week/Day:		
1 piece, 1 cup raw, 1/2 cup canned, 1 oz dried, 6 oz juice						**Fat**	
						Total	

Whole Grains (6-11 servings)					Servings Per Week/Day:		
1 slice bread, 1/2 muffin/bun/bagel/tortilla, 1/2 c. pasta/rice, 1oz b/fast cereal						**Fat**	
						Total	

Meats, Beans, Eggs (2-3 Servings)					Servings Per Week/Day:		
1 egg, 3 oz of meat/fish/poultry, 15 nuts, 1 cup beans						**Fat**	
						Total	

Dairy Products (2-3 servings)					Servings Per Week/Day:		
1 cup milk, 1 oz cheese, 1 cup yogurt						**Fat**	
						Total	

Fats, Oil, Butters (Sparingly)					Servings Per Week/Day:		
1 Tbsp for oils, dressings, mayo, nut butters and butter/margarine						**Fat**	
						Total	

Sweets & Snacks (Sparingly)					Servings Per Week/Day:		
1 piece of candy, 1 serving of fast food, 1 serving of snack foods						**Fat**	
						Total	

Beverages/Water (8-10 cups)					Servings Per Week/Day:		
1 cup of water (Track your soda, coffee, tea, & alcohol calories here)							
						Total	

Difference: _____   Total Calories: _____

Supplements

Mood and Complexion

Mood		Complexion	
Notes:			

Exercise Page - Week Eight - Day 3

Date: _____   Calories Burned: _____

Remember to warm up prior to exercising!

Cardio Training			Strength Training	
Time	Distance	Cal Burn	Time	Increases

Muscle Group	Weight	Repetitions
Upper Body Exercises		
Neck		
Delts (upper arm)		
Traps (Upper back)		
Pecs (chest)		
Biceps (front arm)		
Triceps (back arm)		
Oblique (waist)		
Abs (stomach)		
Lats (middle back)		
Lower Body Exercises		
Lower Back		
Inner Thigh		
Outer Thigh		
Quads (front thigh)		
Gluts (buttocks)		
Hamstring (back thigh)		
Calves (lower back leg)		
Push-ups		
Sit-ups		
Lunges		
Squats		

Diet Page - Week Eight - Day 4

Calorie Intake Required: _____   Date: _____

Fruits (2-4 Servings)					Servings Per Week/Day:			
1 piece, 1/2 cup canned, 1 oz dried, 6 oz juice					Fat Calories			
							Total	

Vegetables (3-5 Servings)					Servings Per Week/Day:			
1 piece, 1 cup raw, 1/2 cup canned, 1 oz dried, 6 oz juice							Fat	
							Total	

Whole Grains (6-11 servings)					Servings Per Week/Day:			
1 slice bread, 1/2 muffin/bun/bagel/tortilla, 1/2 c. pasta/rice, 1oz b/fast cereal							Fat	
							Total	

Meats, Beans, Eggs (2-3 Servings)					Servings Per Week/Day:			
1 egg, 3 oz of meat/fish/poultry, 15 nuts, 1 cup beans							Fat	
							Total	

Dairy Products (2-3 servings)					Servings Per Week/Day:			
1 cup milk, 1 oz cheese, 1 cup yogurt							Fat	
							Total	

Fats, Oil, Butters (Sparingly)					Servings Per Week/Day:			
1 Tbsp for oils, dressings, mayo, nut butters and butter/margarine							Fat	
							Total	

Sweets & Snacks (Sparingly)					Servings Per Week/Day:			
1 piece of candy, 1 serving of fast food, 1 serving of snack foods							Fat	
							Total	

Beverages/Water (8-10 cups)					Servings Per Week/Day:			
1 cup of water (Track your soda, coffee, tea, & alcohol calories here)							Total	

Difference: _____   Total Calories: _____

Supplements

Mood and Complexion

Mood		Complexion	
Notes:			

Exercise Page - Week Eight - Day 4

Date: _____   Calories Burned: _____

Remember to warm up prior to exercising!

Cardio Training			Strength Training	
Time	Distance	Cal Burn	Time	Increases

Muscle Group	Weight	Repetitions
Upper Body Exercises		
Neck		
Delts (upper arm)		
Traps (Upper back)		
Pecs (chest)		
Biceps (front arm)		
Triceps (back arm)		
Oblique (waist)		
Abs (stomach)		
Lats (middle back)		
Lower Body Exercises		
Lower Back		
Inner Thigh		
Outer Thigh		
Quads (front thigh)		
Gluts (buttocks)		
Hamstring (back thigh)		
Calves (lower back leg)		
Push-ups		
Sit-ups		
Lunges		
Squats		

Diet Page - Week Eight - Day 5

Calorie Intake Required: _____   Date: _____

Fruits (2-4 Servings)					Servings Per Week/Day:		
1 piece, 1/2 cup canned, 1 oz dried, 6 oz juice					Fat Calories		
							Total

Vegetables (3-5 Servings)					Servings Per Week/Day:		
1 piece, 1 cup raw, 1/2 cup canned, 1 oz dried, 6 oz juice						Fat	
							Total

Whole Grains (6-11 servings)					Servings Per Week/Day:		
1 slice bread, 1/2 muffin/bun/bagel/tortilla, 1/2 c. pasta/rice, 1oz b/fast cereal						Fat	
							Total

Meats, Beans, Eggs (2-3 Servings)					Servings Per Week/Day:		
1 egg, 3 oz of meat/fish/poultry, 15 nuts, 1 cup beans						Fat	
							Total

Dairy Products (2-3 servings)					Servings Per Week/Day:		
1 cup milk, 1 oz cheese, 1 cup yogurt						Fat	
							Total

Fats, Oil, Butters (Sparingly)					Servings Per Week/Day:		
1 Tbsp for oils, dressings, mayo, nut butters and butter/margarine						Fat	
							Total

Sweets & Snacks (Sparingly)					Servings Per Week/Day:		
1 piece of candy, 1 serving of fast food, 1 serving of snack foods						Fat	
							Total

Beverages/Water (8-10 cups)					Servings Per Week/Day:		
1 cup of water (Track your soda, coffee, tea, & alcohol calories here)							
							Total

Difference: _____   Total Calories: _____

Supplements

Mood and Complexion

Mood		Complexion	
Notes:			

Exercise Page - Week Eight - Day 5

Date: _____   Calories Burned: _____

Remember to warm up prior to exercising!

Cardio Training			Strength Training	
Time	Distance	Cal Burn	Time	Increases

Muscle Group	Weight	Repetitions
Upper Body Exercises		
Neck		
Delts (upper arm)		
Traps (Upper back)		
Pecs (chest)		
Biceps (front arm)		
Triceps (back arm)		
Oblique (waist)		
Abs (stomach)		
Lats (middle back)		
Lower Body Exercises		
Lower Back		
Inner Thigh		
Outer Thigh		
Quads (front thigh)		
Gluts (buttocks)		
Hamstring (back thigh)		
Calves (lower back leg)		
Push-ups		
Sit-ups		
Lunges		
Squats		

Diet Page - Week Eight - Day 6

Calorie Intake Required: _____   Date: _____

Fruits (2-4 Servings)						Servings Per Week/Day:				
1 piece, 1/2 cup canned, 1 oz dried, 6 oz juice						Fat Calories				
									Total	

Vegetables (3-5 Servings)						Servings Per Week/Day:				
1 piece, 1 cup raw, 1/2 cup canned, 1 oz dried, 6 oz juice								Fat		
									Total	

Whole Grains (6-11 servings)						Servings Per Week/Day:				
1 slice bread, 1/2 muffin/bun/bagel/tortilla, 1/2 c. pasta/rice, 1oz b/fast cereal								Fat		
									Total	

Meats, Beans, Eggs (2-3 Servings)						Servings Per Week/Day:				
1 egg, 3 oz of meat/fish/poultry, 15 nuts, 1 cup beans								Fat		
									Total	

Dairy Products (2-3 servings)						Servings Per Week/Day:				
1 cup milk, 1 oz cheese, 1 cup yogurt								Fat		
									Total	

Fats, Oil, Butters (Sparingly)						Servings Per Week/Day:				
1 Tbsp for oils, dressings, mayo, nut butters and butter/margarine								Fat		
									Total	

Sweets & Snacks (Sparingly)						Servings Per Week/Day:				
1 piece of candy, 1 serving of fast food, 1 serving of snack foods								Fat		
									Total	

Beverages/Water (8-10 cups)						Servings Per Week/Day:				
1 cup of water (Track your soda, coffee, tea, & alcohol calories here)										
									Total	

Difference: _____   Total Calories: _____

Supplements

Mood and Complexion

Mood		Complexion	
Notes:			

Exercise Page - Week Eight - Day 6

Date: _____   Calories Burned: _____

Remember to warm up prior to exercising!

Cardio Training			Strength Training	
Time	Distance	Cal Burn	Time	Increases

Muscle Group	Weight	Repetitions
Upper Body Exercises		
Neck		
Delts (upper arm)		
Traps (Upper back)		
Pecs (chest)		
Biceps (front arm)		
Triceps (back arm)		
Oblique (waist)		
Abs (stomach)		
Lats (middle back)		
Lower Body Exercises		
Lower Back		
Inner Thigh		
Outer Thigh		
Quads (front thigh)		
Gluts (buttocks)		
Hamstring (back thigh)		
Calves (lower back leg)		
Push-ups		
Sit-ups		
Lunges		
Squats		

Diet Page - Week Eight - Day 7

Calorie Intake Required: _____   Date: _____

Fruits (2-4 Servings)					Servings Per Week/Day:			
1 piece, 1/2 cup canned, 1 oz dried, 6 oz juice					**Fat Calories**			
							Total	

Vegetables (3-5 Servings)					Servings Per Week/Day:			
1 piece, 1 cup raw, 1/2 cup canned, 1 oz dried, 6 oz juice							Fat	
							Total	

Whole Grains (6-11 servings)					Servings Per Week/Day:			
1 slice bread, 1/2 muffin/bun/bagel/tortilla, 1/2 c. pasta/rice, 1oz b/fast cereal							Fat	
							Total	

Meats,Beans, Eggs (2-3 Servings)					Servings Per Week/Day:			
1 egg, 3 oz of meat/fish/poultry, 15 nuts, 1 cup beans							Fat	
							Total	

Dairy Products (2-3 servings)					Servings Per Week/Day:			
1 cup milk, 1 oz cheese, 1 cup yogurt							Fat	
							Total	

Fats, Oil, Butters (Sparingly)					Servings Per Week/Day:			
1 Tbsp for oils, dressings, mayo, nut butters and butter/margarine							Fat	
							Total	

Sweets & Snacks (Sparingly)					Servings Per Week/Day:			
1 piece of candy, 1 serving of fast food, 1 serving of snack foods							Fat	
							Total	

Beverages/Water (8-10 cups)					Servings Per Week/Day:			
1 cup of water (Track your soda, coffee, tea, & alcohol calories here)								
							Total	

Difference: _____   Total Calories: _____

Supplements

Mood and Complexion

Mood		Complexion	
Notes:			

Exercise Page - Week Eight - Day 7

Date: _____   Calories Burned: _____

Remember to warm up prior to exercising!

Cardio Training			Strength Training	
Time	Distance	Cal Burn	Time	Increases

Muscle Group	Weight	Repetitions
Upper Body Exercises		
Neck		
Delts (upper arm)		
Traps (Upper back)		
Pecs (chest)		
Biceps (front arm)		
Triceps (back arm)		
Oblique (waist)		
Abs (stomach)		
Lats (middle back)		
Lower Body Exercises		
Lower Back		
Inner Thigh		
Outer Thigh		
Quads (front thigh)		
Gluts (buttocks)		
Hamstring (back thigh)		
Calves (lower back leg)		
Push-ups		
Sit-ups		
Lunges		
Squats		

You're Done!

Take a picture!

If you have completed the eight weeks in this notebook, you are well on your way to keeping the habit of a healthy lifestyle. You can continue without the aid of **The Workout Notebook** or go get yourself another one! Either way, the best improvements of your body are still to come. If you continue, weeks 8-12 are the best for noticing significant differences.

Table of Calories

Food Group	Description	Serving Size	Calories	Fat Calories
Beverage	Liquor, 80 proof	2 oz.	130	
Beverage	Beer	12 ox.	160	
Beverage	Mountain Dew	1 each	170	
Beverage	Wine	4 oz.	110	
Fruit	Apple	1 each	80	
Fruit	Apple Juice	1 cup	120	
Fruit	Banana	1 each	100	
Fruit	Cantaloupe	1 cup	80	
Fruit	Grapes, Green	10 each	35	
Fruit	Orange Juice	1 cup	110	
Fruit	Peach	1 each	10	
Fruit	Pear, Bartlett	1 each	100	
Fruit	Raisins	1/2 cup	210	
Fruit	Strawberries	1 cup	55	
Fruit	Tomato Juice	6 oz.	35	
Fruit	Tomatoes	1 each	25	
Milk Product	Cheddar Cheese	2 oz.	230	
Milk Product	Ice Cream	1 cup	270	
Milk Product	Milk, Fat-free	1 cup	90	
Milk Product	Milk, Whole	1 cup	150	
Milk Product	Yogurt, Low Fat	1 cup	145	
Meat Etc.	Bacon	2 slices	85	
Meat Etc.	Beefsteak, broiled, lean	4 oz.	230	
Meat Etc.	Chicken, Broiled	6 oz.	240	
Meat Etc.	Crabmeat	1 cup	135	
Meat Etc.	Egg	1 each	80	
Meat Etc.	Halibut, broiled	4 oz.	195	
Meat Etc.	Ham	4 oz.	245	
Meat Etc.	Hot dog	1 each	170	
Meat Etc.	Lamb Roast	4 oz.	315	
Meat Etc.	Salami	2 oz.	235	
Meat Etc.	Salmon, Canned	1/2 cup	90	
Meat Etc.	Shrimp	4 oz.	105	
Meat Etc.	Tuna	2 oz.	60	
Meat Etc.	Turkey, Roasted Dark	4 oz.	175	
Meat Etc.	Turkey, Roasted White	4 oz.	150	
Meat Etc.	Veal Chop, loin	4 oz.	265	

Food Group	Description	Serving Size	Calories	Fat Calories
Sweets Etc.	Brownie	1 each	95	
Sweets Etc.	Pie, Apple	1 slice	405	
Sweets Etc.	Pie, Pecan	1 slice	580	
Sweets Etc.	Pie, Pumpkin	1 slice	325	
Sweets Etc.	Potato Chips	1 oz.	160	
Spreads	Butter	1 Tbsp	100	
Spreads	Dressing, Catalina Fat Free	1 Tbsp	35	
Spreads	Dressing, Italian Fat Free	1 Tbsp	15	
Spreads	Dressing, Thousand Island	1 Tbsp	90	
Spreads	Honey	1 Tbsp	65	
Spreads	Jam	1 Tbsp	55	
Spreads	Ketchup	1 Tbsp	15	
Spreads	Mayonnaise	1 Tbsp	100	
Spreads	Oil, Vegetable	1 Tbsp	120	
Spreads	Peanut Butter	1 Tbsp	105	
Spreads	Sugar, white	1 Tbsp	45	
Vegetable	Asparagus	1 cup	30	
Vegetable	Beans, Green	1 cup	30	
Vegetable	Beans, Kidney	1 cup	220	
Vegetable	Beans, Lima	1 cup	160	
Vegetable	Beans, Pinto	1/2 cup	110	
Vegetable	Beets	1 cup	60	
Vegetable	Broccoli	1 cup	40	
Vegetable	Cabbage, Cooked	1 cup	30	
Vegetable	Cabbage, Raw	1 cup	22	
Vegetable	Carrots	1 cup	50	
Vegetable	Celery	1 cup	20	
Vegetable	Corn	1/2 cup	90	
Vegetable	Lettuce, Iceberg	1 head	70	
Vegetable	Mushrooms	1 cup	20	
Vegetable	Olives	2 oz.	25	
Vegetable	Peas	1/2 cup	60	
Vegetable	Potato, baked	1 each	100	
Vegetable	Potato, fried	10 each	135	
Vegetable	Radishes, Raw	1/2 cup	5	
Vegetable	Spinach	1 cup	35	
Vegetable	Squash, Acorn baked	1 cup	110	

Food Group	Description	Serving Size	Calories	Fat Calories
Vegetable	Squash, Summer	1 cup	30	
Whole Grain	Almonds	1/2 cup	345	
Whole Grain	Bread, Rye	1 slice	60	
Whole Grain	Bread, Wheat	1 slice	65	
Whole Grain	Bread, White	1 slice	70	
Whole Grain	Cheerios	1/2 cup	150	
Whole Grain	Corn Chips	1 cup	140	
Whole Grain	Crackers	1 each	12	
Whole Grain	Croutons	2 oz.	30	
Whole Grain	Mac & Cheese	1 cup	410	
Whole Grain	Muffin, Blueberry	1 each	170	
Whole Grain	Noodles	1 cup	210	
Whole Grain	Oatmeal	1/2 cup	150	
Whole Grain	Pancake	1 each	150	
Whole Grain	Pizza, Cheese	1 slice	145	
Whole Grain	Rice, Cooked	1 cup	225	
Whole Grain	Spaghetti, al dente	1 cup	190	
Whole Grain	Spaghetti, tender	1 cup	155	

Table of Activity

Activity for 1 hour	130lbs	155lbs	190lbs
Aerobics	354	422	548
Aerobics, high	413	493	604
Aerobics, low	295	352	431
Backpacking	413	493	604
Basketball, shooting	266	317	388
Bike Riding - <10 mph	236	281	345
Bike Riding – 20 mph	944	1126	1380
BMX Racing	502	598	733
Stationary Bike	295	352	431
Stationary Bike – light	325	387	474
Stationary Bike – moderate	413	493	604
Stationary Bike – vigorous	738	880	1078
Bowling	177	211	259
Calisthenics – vigorous	472	563	690
Calisthenics – at home	236	281	345
Cleaning house – general	148	176	216
Coaching a sport	325	287	474
Dancing – general	148	176	216
Football/Baseball – catch	531	633	776
Frisbee	207	246	302
Gardening	325	387	474
Golf – general	177	211	259
Handball – general	472	563	690
Health club exercise	354	422	518
Hiking cross country	472	563	690
Ice Hockey	354	422	518
Horseback Riding	384	457	561
Hunting	708	844	1035
Jogging	590	704	863
Judo, karate, kick boxing	295	352	431
Mowing the lawn	148	176	216
Racquetball	236	281	345
Rope jumping – general	561	669	819
Stationary Rowing – general	502	598	733
Running – general	590	704	863

Power Foods

The information for this section is from <u>Muscle & Fitness</u>, October 1999, pages 71-73.

Food	Serving Size	Calories	Protein in Grams	Carbs in Grams	Fat in Grams
Whole Egg	1	76	6.5	.6	5 g
Egg White	1	16	3.5	.3	0
Top Sirloin	3-1/2 oz	199	28	0	9
Oatmeal	1 cup	145	6	25	2
Spaghetti, Sauce & Lean Beef	1 cup	437	33	51	11
Grape Nuts	1/2 c	210	6	47	1
M&F Hero Sandwich	1	339	27	41	7
Chicken Breast	3-1/2 oz	165	31	0	4
Apricots, Fresh	3	54	1.5	12	Trace
Apricots, Dried	1/4 c	84	1	20	Trace
Apricots, Canned	1/2 c	64	1	15	Trace
Sweet Potato	4 oz	117	2	28	Trace
Canned Tuna	3-1/2 oz	116	26	0	1
Protein Powder	1 oz	100	24	0	0
Apple	1	81	Trace	21	Trace
Yogurt, Plain	8 oz	127	13	17	Trace
Kiwi	1	46	Trace	11	Trace
Pizza, Tombstone Light Supreme	138 g	270	25	30	9
Orange Juice	1 c	105	2	24	Trace
Blueberries	1 c	80	1	19	1
Carb-Protein Drink	20 oz	400	20	60	9
Peanuts, no salt	1 oz	178	7	6	14
Water	1 c	0	0	0	0

Place Your Before Picture Here:

Place Your After Picture Here: